All That You Need To Know About Google Keep for Increasing Productivity

Koushik K

Published by Koushik K, 2017.

While every precaution has been taken in the preparation of this book, the publisher assumes no responsibility for errors or omissions, or for damages resulting from the use of the information contained herein.

ALL THAT YOU NEED TO KNOW ABOUT GOOGLE KEEP FOR INCREASING PRODUCTIVITY

First edition. March 17, 2017.

Copyright © 2017 Koushik K.

ISBN: 979-8201011369

Written by Koushik K.

Table of Contents

What is Google Keep

Google Keep is a note-taking service developed by Google. Google Keep is available as a mobile app for the Android and iOS mobile operating systems and as a web application.

This is not only a note taking application but it is also used to set reminders. The app is also used to make your notes colorful and decorated with images. You can categorize the notes into various categories using labels.

You can also use hash tags, save web links etc. you can use these hash tags for easy searching of your notes.

There are many advantages in this service of Google which will be explained in detail throughout this book.

How can it benefit Authors and Business people

Though this book is useful for anyone and everyone who wants to use Google keep for increasing their productivity, the examples used involve how an author or business person would use it.

You may be wondering what does Google keep offer authors and business people. Why did I choose to write about Google keep for authors and businesses? Google keep can be used by students, teachers, professionals of any kind, and anyone who wants to take notes. Right?

Yes. You guessed right, anyone can use it to take notes and set reminders. There are two important reasons for telling that Google keep is good for authors and businesses.

I am an author and an internet marketer. In this book I will explain how I use Google keep to keep me organized and improve my productivity

The second reason is, anyone can take notes but for professionals I personally feel it's very important for them to use Google keep and it is definitely a life changer.

Authors can be 200% more productive by following the schedule correctly and setting their realistic writing goals.

Business people have many appointments, meet-ups and targets. By using Google keep, they can make sure they don't miss an appointment; they don't skip an important task which can cause them loss in business.

I am going to use my writing schedule and my internet marketing tasks as an example but you can use similar techniques for increasing productivity in any profession or business.

Why Google keep?

Nowadays we all use a note-taking application for one purpose or the other. What is so special in Google keep?

Google keep is everywhere

You can access your notes everywhere. In your PC, laptop computer, Mobile, etc. You have 24x7 access of your notes; all you need is an internet connection. You don't even have to have your own devices. You can access it from any place you have access to internet.

Security

We all trust in security of Google. In my opinion it's even more secure than your PC. Your only responsibility would be to keep your password a secret.

Searching and sorting features

We all know the power of Google's search feature and its speed. So Google keep can beat any other note taking apps in this. You definitely know this already. The labels feature which we have in Gmail is also available here with a mild difference in the look and feel.

Hash tags

The ability to add different hashtags in a note and use them to find the notes makes is even easier to sort and search.

Setting reminders

Google keep not only works as a note taking app but also reminds us to check out the notes from time to time. This feature is very useful for sticking to the schedule even when we are busy doing some other work which may be interesting for us.

There are other cool features like you can dictate your notes, you can send your notes to Google docs, you can share them with whomever you wish to etc

Signing in to Google keep

As with any other Google apps or services, you just need a Gmail account to login to your keep

Go to https://www.google.com/keep/

Click try Google keep you will get four options

Android, IOS, chrome and web

Let us start with web.

To access keep from the web go to http://keep.google.com

Just login with your Gmail account (if not already logged in)

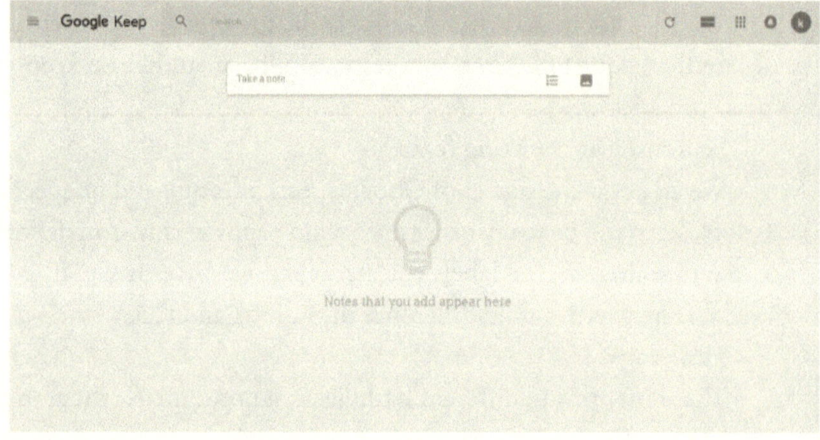

First time view of Google keep account

The yellow bar contains a few icons. Let me explain them now

The toggle menu button makes the right side menu visible or hidden.

The search bar is used to search by entering keyword, queries or hash tags

The refresh button is used to reload the page (the app).

ALL THAT YOU NEED TO KNOW ABOUT GOOGLE KEEP FOR INCREASING PRODUCTIVITY

The toggle view button is used to switch between two kinds of views (grid view and list view).

You can also install the android app of Google keep, if you prefer your smart phone for work and note taking. I find it comfortable to use my Laptop for taking notes than my mobile. I have also installed the android app though.

Let's start using Google keep to take notes in the next chapter.

Taking Notes

To take a note, click in the text box which says take a note and start typing

See you have two icons to the left corner, a list icon and an image icon

I will explain about it a bit later in this chapter

Once you click the text take a note, the box will expand as shown below

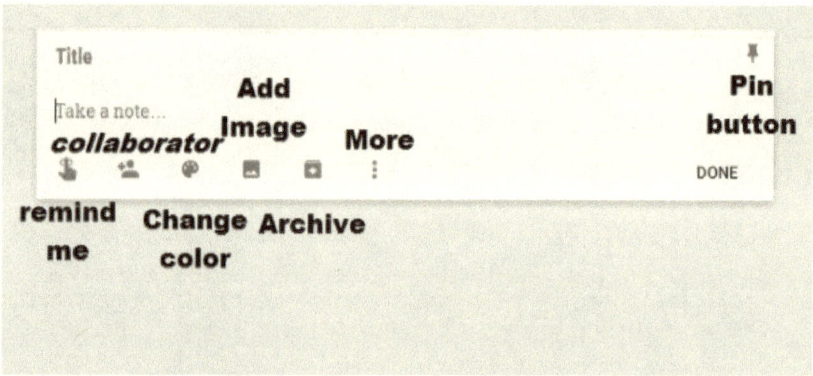

You can type the title of the note you are taking.

Then type whatever notes you want to take.

The pin button in the top left corner of this box is used to pin your important note in the top so that you won't lose it even after you take many other notes which are less important.

The first icon in the bottom left corner which looks like a small hand is the remind me button. I will explain in detail in a separate chapter because, it is one of the important features of keep.

Sharing

The man icon with a plus sign is the collaborator Icon. It is used to share your note with anyone you want.

Click that icon and you will see the sharing box appear

It will show your email address and in the field next to it you can type the name of any contact from your Google contacts list or directly type in the email address of anyone you want to share the particular note with.

You can add multiple email addresses by adding a comma after every email.

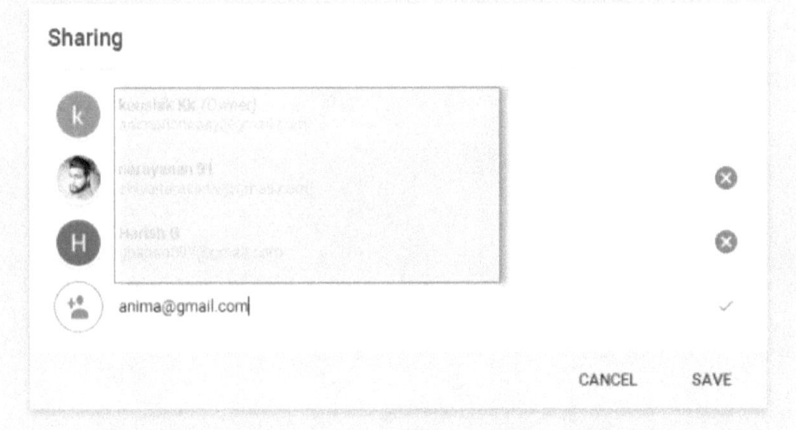

You can also click the tick mark button to add an email address to the sharing list.

After you are done with adding email addresses you can click change.

You can use the x mark button to remove the emails you have already added.

You can add or remove email addresses later by going to the same note again and then clicking the collaborator icon.

Change color

The color palette icon is used to give a background color for the note. This makes your notes look interesting, unique and colorful.

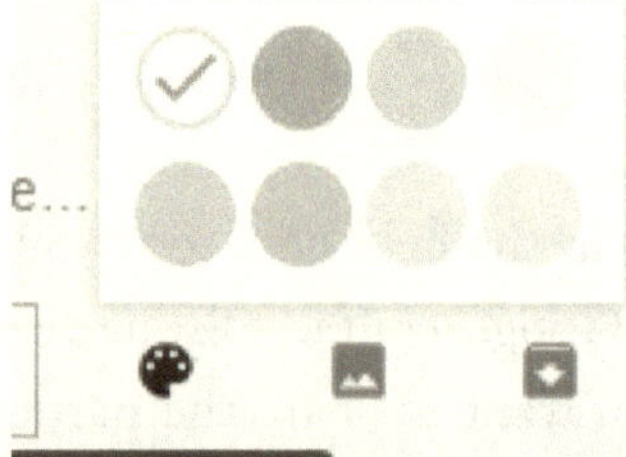

Click any color you want and then the note's background color will change

Image

The image icon is to add images to the note

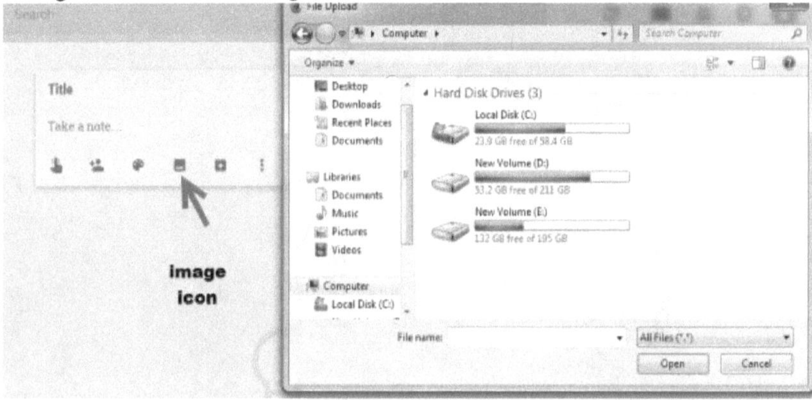

Browse for any image and click open. The image will be uploaded (may take a few seconds to a minute depending on your internet's speed)

You will see the image on top of your note after it is uploaded. You can also upload multiple images by using the image icon.

You can delete the images using the bin icon you see in the bottom left corner of the image.

Find images by searching the text in it

If you have saved some text in the form of images, you can type in some words from the text and find the images

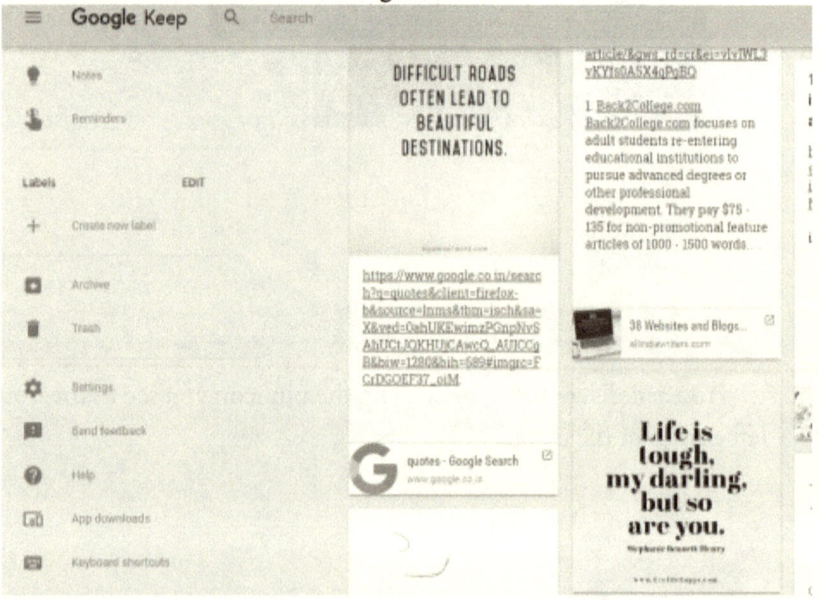

See I have two images in my goggle keep

I am going to show you that you can search for text within images

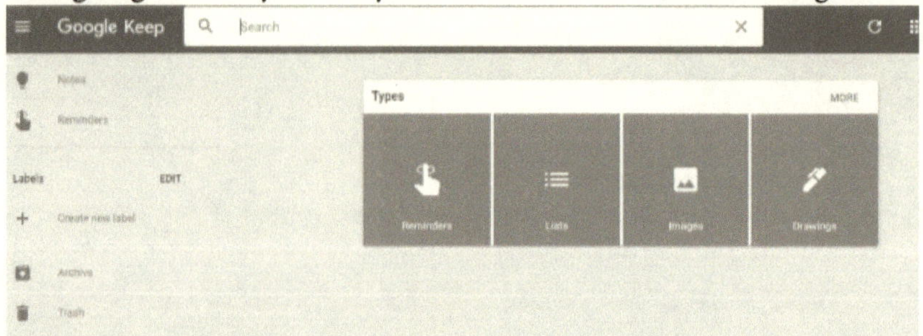

I clicked the search bar and this above screen appeared.

I started searching for the word beauty. I typed beau. And see the magic.

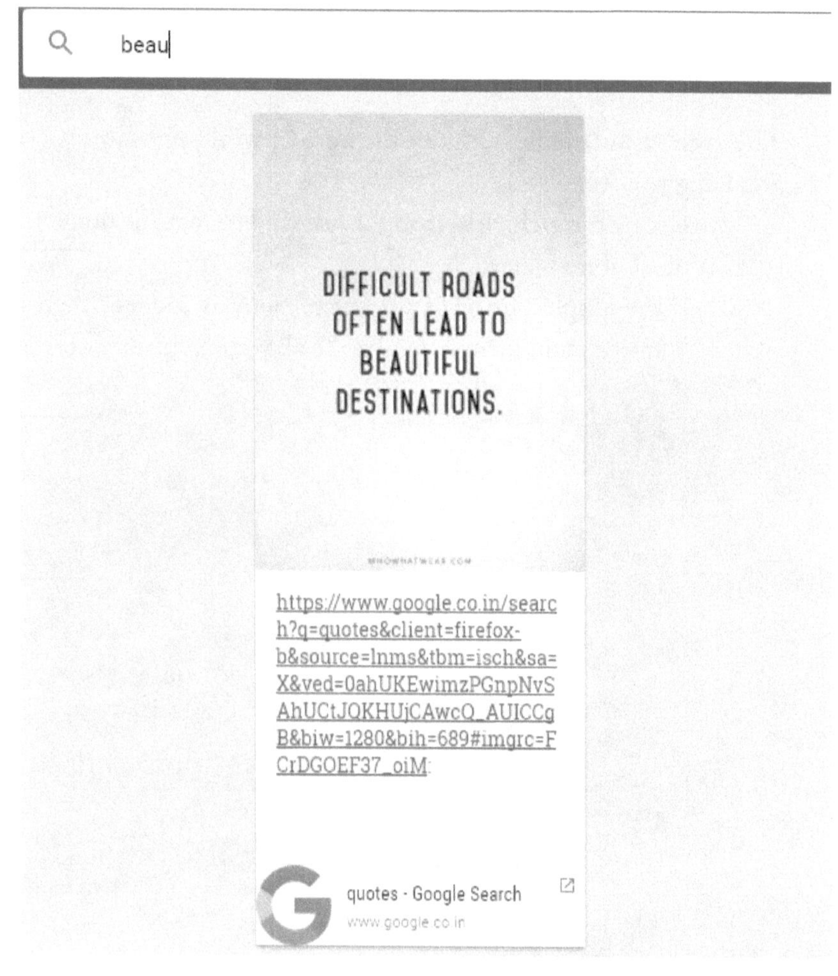
beau
DIFFICULT ROADS
OFTEN LEAD TO
BEAUTIFUL
DESTINATIONS.
https://www.google.co.in/searc
h?q=quotes&client=firefox-
b&source=lnms&tbm=isch&sa=
X&ved=0ahUKEwimzPGnpNvS
AhUCtJQKHUjCAwcQ_AUICCg
B&biw=1280&bih=689#imgrc=F
CrDGOEF37_oiM:
quotes - Google Search
www.google.co.in

Archive

The archive button is to archive the note (it works in a same way as in archiving your emails)

By clicking the archive button the note hides from the home screen (the list of all notes taken)

Click the toggle button if the main menu is hidden, then click archive from the main menu. You can see all your archived notes there.

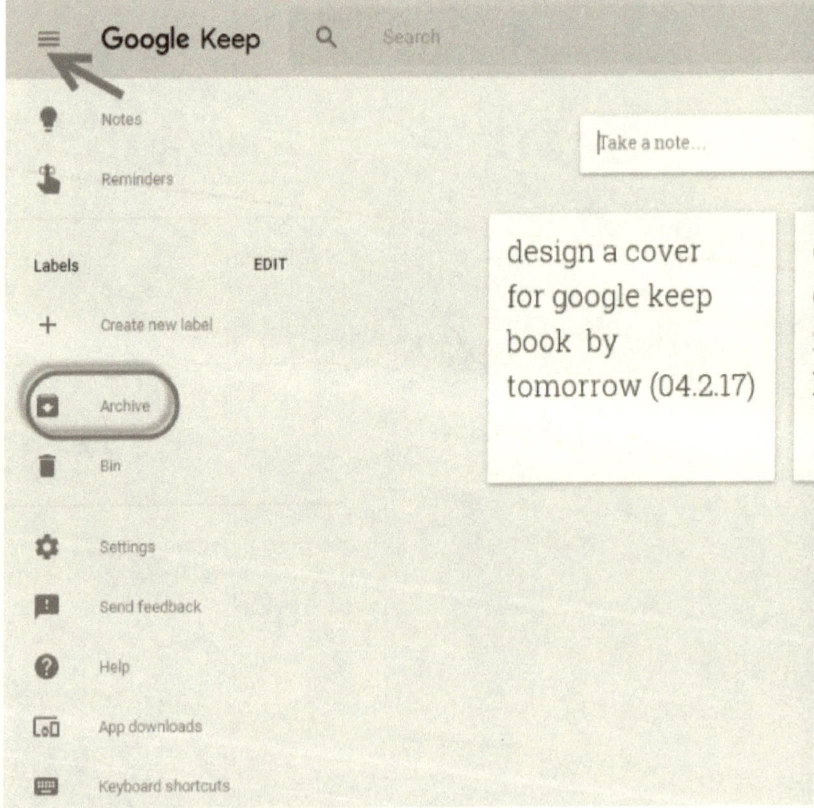

More options

The three vertical dots are the more options icon.

The more options menu has many options. Let me explain one by one

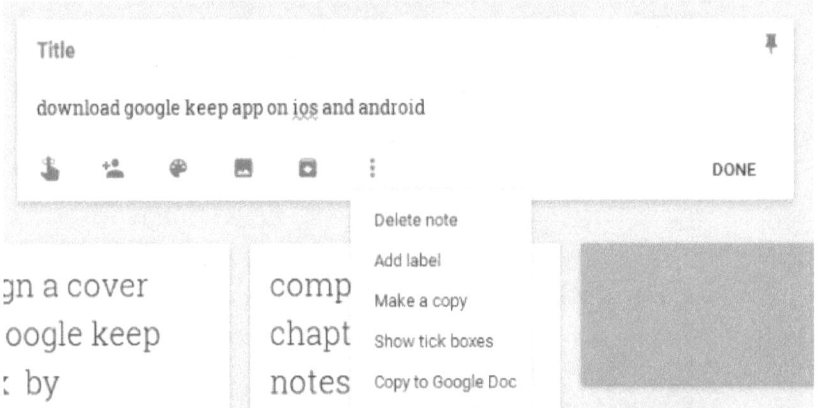

Delete note: you can delete the note using that button. (Delete it only if you no longer need it) you can always archive your note instead of deleting.

Add label: The label is a way you can categorize your notes by different topics or categories. You can add multiple labels to a note.

Make a copy: used to duplicate a note and then you can edit it to add more details. This is useful when you have to take notes of similar things.

Clicking show tick boxes will turn your note in to a list of tasks with tick boxes. You can click the tick boxes after you complete that task.

Copy to Google doc is used to export the note to a Google doc

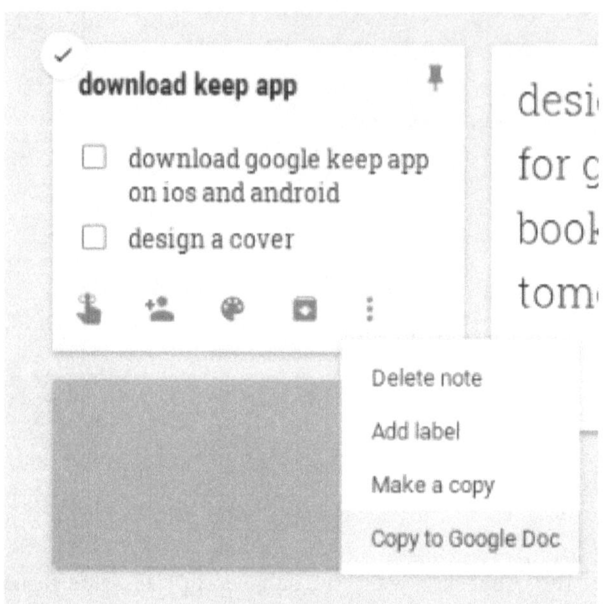

To make a copy of the note in Google doc click more options button and then click copy to Google Doc

A notification will appear as shown below

Then the below notification will appear in the bottom of the screen
\

Click OPEN DOC to view your document in Google doc

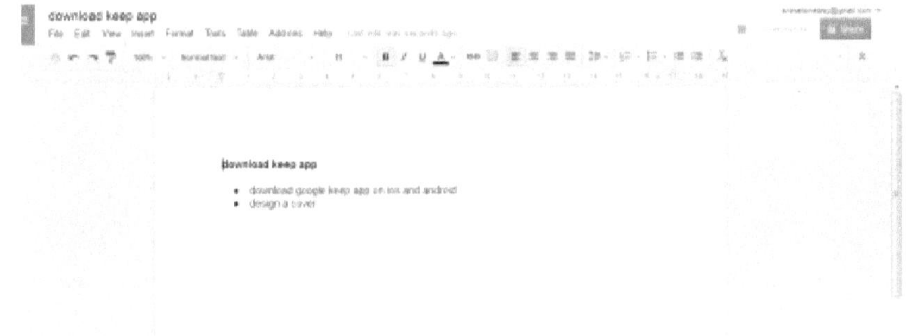

Now that we know what are the options and different features give in a note,

We can see how to edit or delete a note you already took.

Editing a note

To edit a note just click on the note and it will turn editable.

Deleting a note

Click more options and then click Delete note. The note will be moved to bin. The note stays in the bin for seven days and then it gets deleted permanently

You can see the notes in the bin by clicking the bin button in the main menu.

From the bin you can delete the deleted notes permanently or you can restore them by clicking the vertical dots button (shown below

download keep app

download google keep app on ios and android

design a cover

Delete forever

Restore

You also have an EMPTY RECYCLEBIN NOW link in the bin. You can use it to permanently clear the recycle bin whenever you want.

The hidden features

1. If you add a web URL (website address) to your note. It automatically turns in to a clickable hyperlink

2. You can use hashtags to create labels

I will give you an exercise in the end of each chapter so that you can follow along with me. This will be very useful for you to learn using Google keep in a step by step way.

Exercise

Create a note,
> Change the color of the note
> Add a relevant image to your note.

Setting Reminders

Now that you know how to take notes let's start setting reminders. In my opinion this is the most useful feature of Google keep.

Now that you may have created some notes, if you followed with me. You can set a reminder to it. If you haven't created any notes yet, create a note first and follow along with me.

Login to your Google keep

Click the set reminder icon in any note you wish to set the reminder for (remind me icon is marked in the below screenshot)

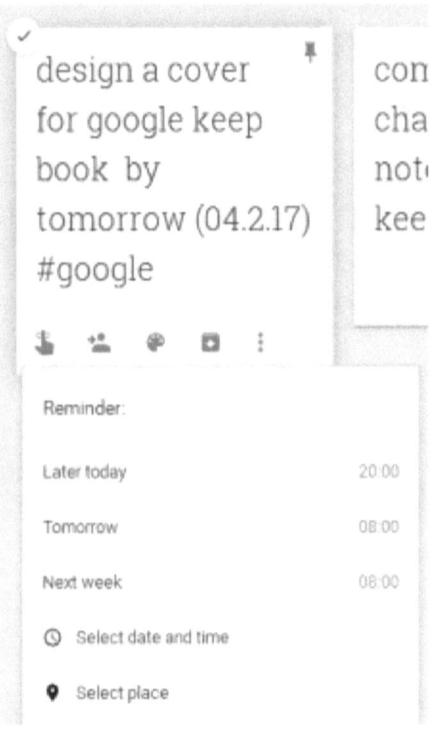

You will see the reminder options appear
You can either click later today, tomorrow or next week

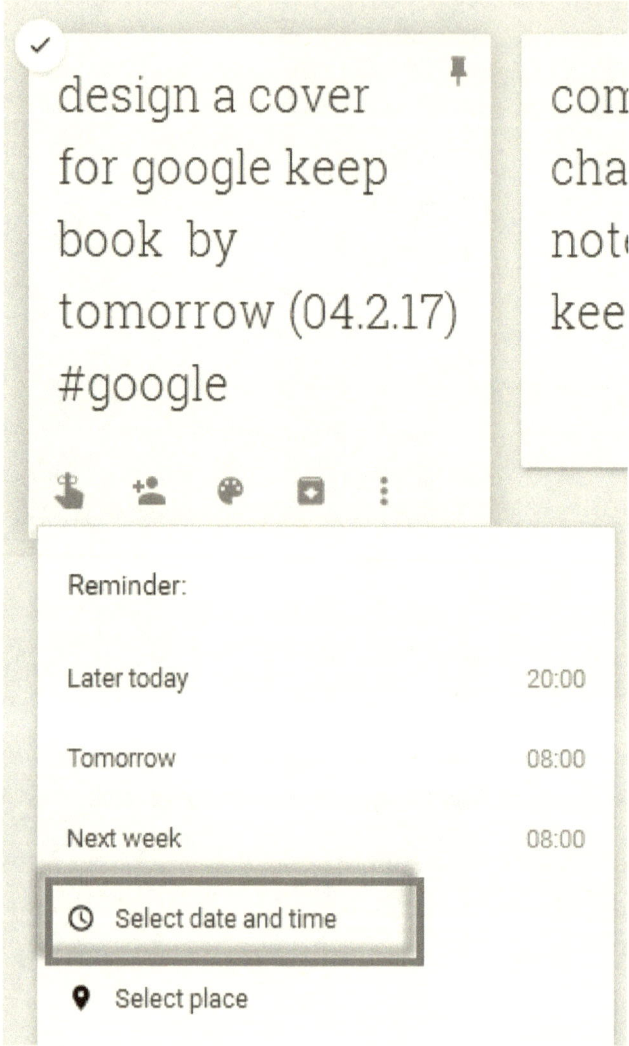

If you want to be more precise you can click select date and time (that's what I like to do because I like very precise reminders)

As you can see in the above example, my note is to design a cover for my book, I set the exact time when I plan to start my cover designing in the date and time. Since I know I will be sitting before my computer, all I need is a reminder to remind me to start the work and

I will immediately start it I will pause the writing or any other job I am doing and go to the design job.

You may think that is insane, but it works out for me. I am a non fiction writer (as you already know) and I don't have to worry much about moods or creativity and stick to my schedule easily.

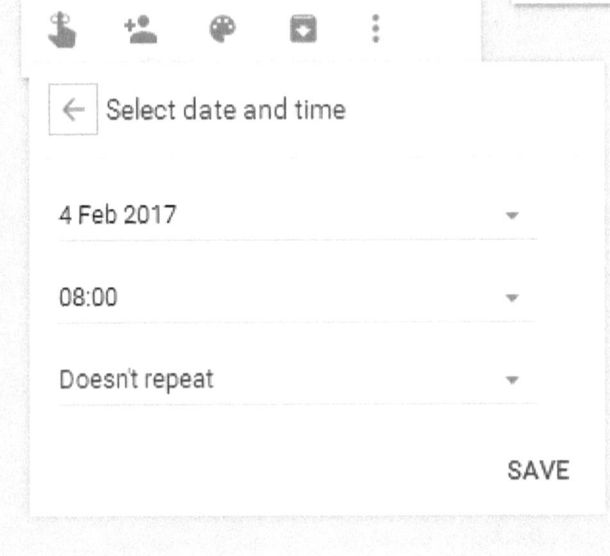

Now we can set the date time and reminder type from here.

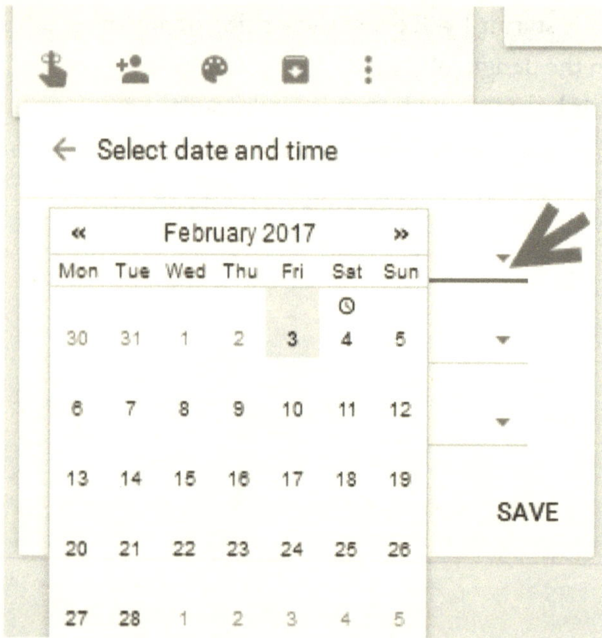

First you should select a date from the date picker

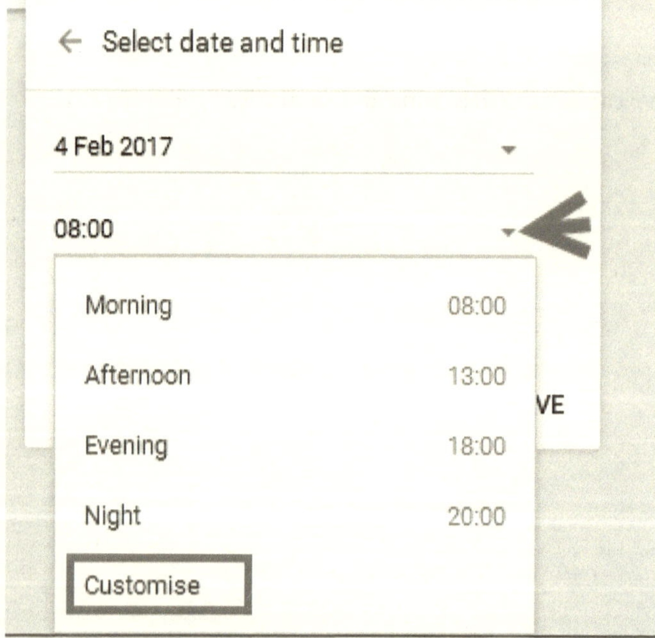

ALL THAT YOU NEED TO KNOW ABOUT GOOGLE KEEP FOR INCREASING PRODUCTIVITY

The next step is to select time; you can select morning, afternoon etc (I will show you how to change the default timing for morning, afternoon etc in a later chapter)

As I already told you I like everything to be precise so I click customize

Then type in a precise timing and save it

The next step is to set the reminder type. The default is doesn't repeat (because most of the notes doesn't need regular reminders

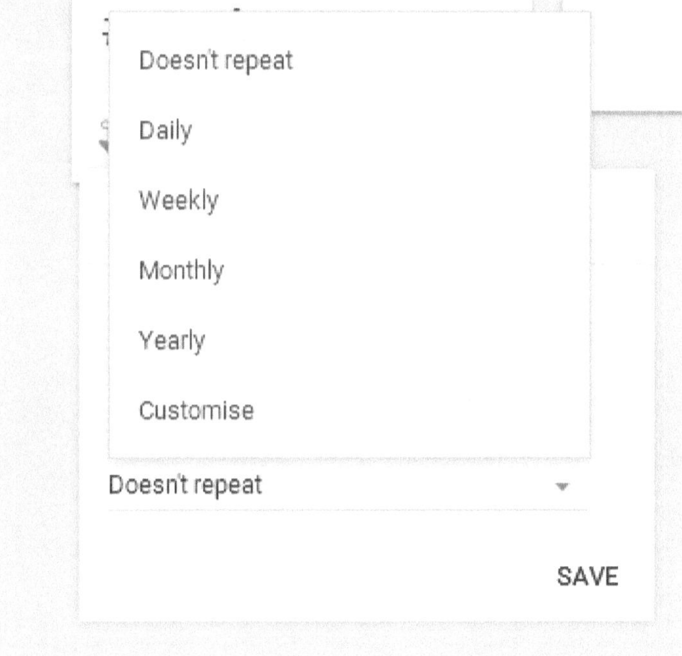

You can change it to daily, if the note is your daily routine, or weekly if it is your weekly ritual, etc. yearly reminders are useful for festival dates, book release dates etc

You can also customize the reminder if you want.

Do you know: The reminder will also appear in Google Now as well as in Google Inbox, if you use it—and marking it as done in any of those places will cause it to be dismissed everywhere.

You can always click the main menu toggle button and then click reminders, to see the upcoming reminders.

Pinning Important Notes or Tasks

There is really nothing much to explain but I find it important so I am dedicating a separate chapter for the topic.

We may have a certain number of notes, we need to see daily. A daily routine or schedule for example. The creative hours which you want to sit for writing. Or even some inspiration words about your ambition or dream with a wonderful image which will cheer you up.

The choices are endless. I recommend you do something like that, that greatly improves your productivity.

You can also set a reminder to that note to remind you every day in the morning so you never fail to look at it.

This really helps me very much as a writer to stick to my schedule.

This is what I use

You can do something similar

Pinned

- [ ] start writing by 9 AM
- [ ] Never stop till 11 AM (you may choose to write about different...
- [ ] Take a 15-20 Min Break
- [ ] Start writing before 11:30 AM
- [ ] stop at 1 PM (lunch time)
- [ ] start your Design works by 2PM
- [ ] start editing and proof reading by 4 30 PM
- [ ] go for a walk by 6 PM

Keyboard shortcuts to speed it up a little

Navigation

    j / k : Navigate to next/previous note

    n / p : Navigate to next/previous list item

    Application

    c : Compose a new note

    l : Compose a new list

    / : Search notes

    <Ctrl> + a : Select all notes

    ? : Open keyboard shortcut help

    @ : Send feedback

    Actions

    e : Archive note

    # : Delete note

    x : Select note

    <Ctrl> + g : Toggle between list and grid view

    Editor

    <ESC> : Finish editing

    <Ctrl> + Enter : Finish editing

    <Ctrl> + Shift + 8 : Toggle checkboxes

Settings (from browser)

Go to keep.google.com[1] and login
Click the main menu toggle button
Then click settings

Settings

List behaviour

Add new items to the bottom ☑

Move ticked items to bottom ☑

Customise your reminder defaults

Morning   08:00

Afternoon   13:00

Evening   18:00

Enable sharing ☑

Display rich link previews ☑

CANCEL   SAVE

You can leave everything to default (as ticked)

---

1. http://keep.google.com/

ALL THAT YOU NEED TO KNOW ABOUT GOOGLE KEEP FOR INCREASING PRODUCTIVITY

Everything is self explanatory and hence I am not telling you explicitly.

The only thing you may wish to change would be your morning, afternoon and evening time.

Change it to your desired timing and then click save.

Installing Google keep in all your devices

Though we have used a browser to explore Google keep, there are many additional features which you get through to android app and chrome extension.

I recommend you to install Google keep in all your different devices so that you don't need a browser to check your notes. You can check your notes from your android or iOS app also.

I personally like to use Firefox browser for using the internet in my pc and laptop but I also have a chrome browser because I like some of the extensions and apps that are only available in chrome. Google keep is one of them.

To install apps in Google chrome, open your Google chrome browser and login to Google keep.

Click the main menu toggle button if the main menu is hidden.

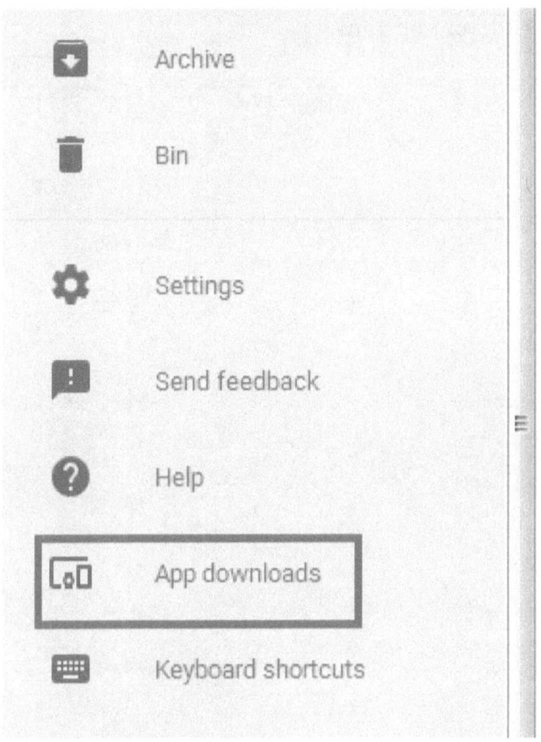

Scroll down a bit and click app downloads.
A new tab will open.

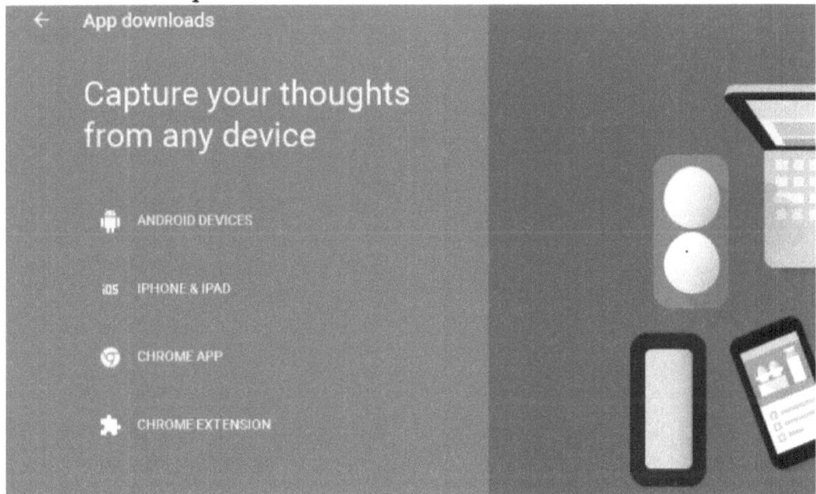

It will show you different options.

Google Keep Chrome app

Click chrome app

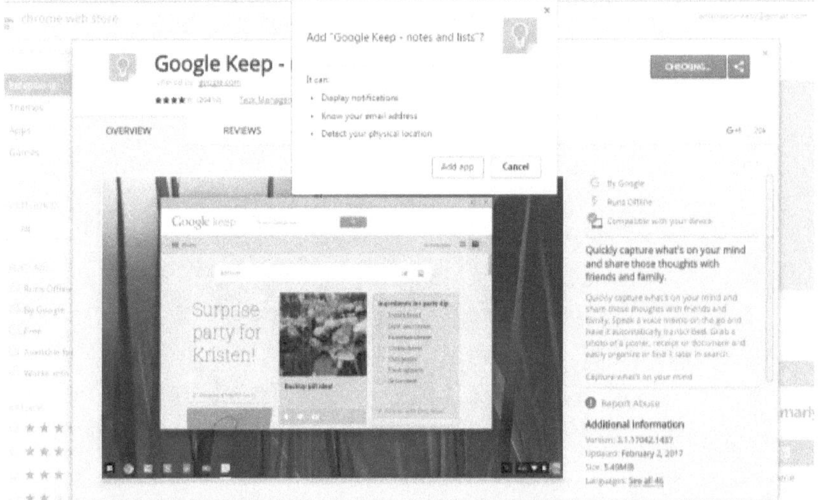

A Google chrome app page will popup, click install and then a small window will popup. Click add app.

Wait a few seconds the app will be installed

Go to app downloads page again from Google keep,

Google Keep Chrome extension

Click CHROME EXTENSION

The Google keep chrome extension page will appear.

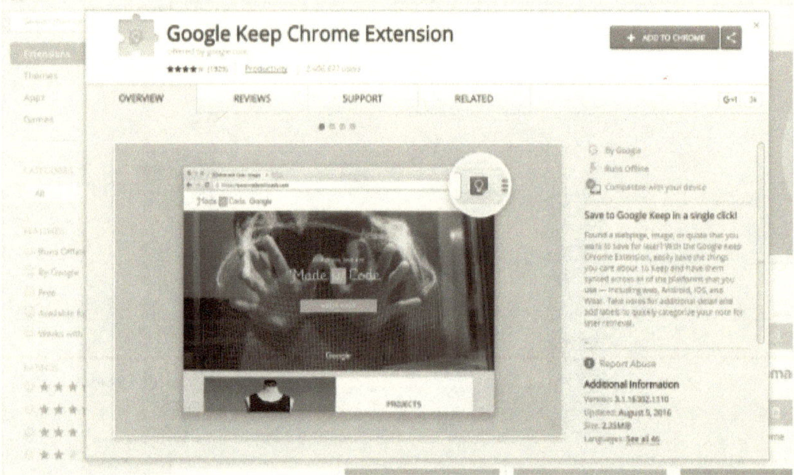

Click add extension

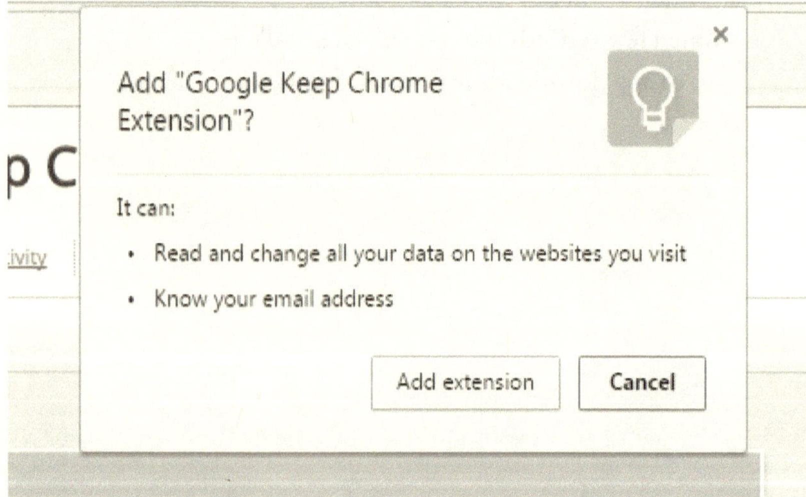

Click add extension.
Wait for the extension to install.

Installing the android app

I recommend you to download the Google keep android app from your android smart phone by going to Google play and searching for Google keep.

Install the app. I personally don't use an iOS app. If you want you can use it too.

Open your Google play store in your android mobile.

Search for Google keep and tap it to visit the app page.

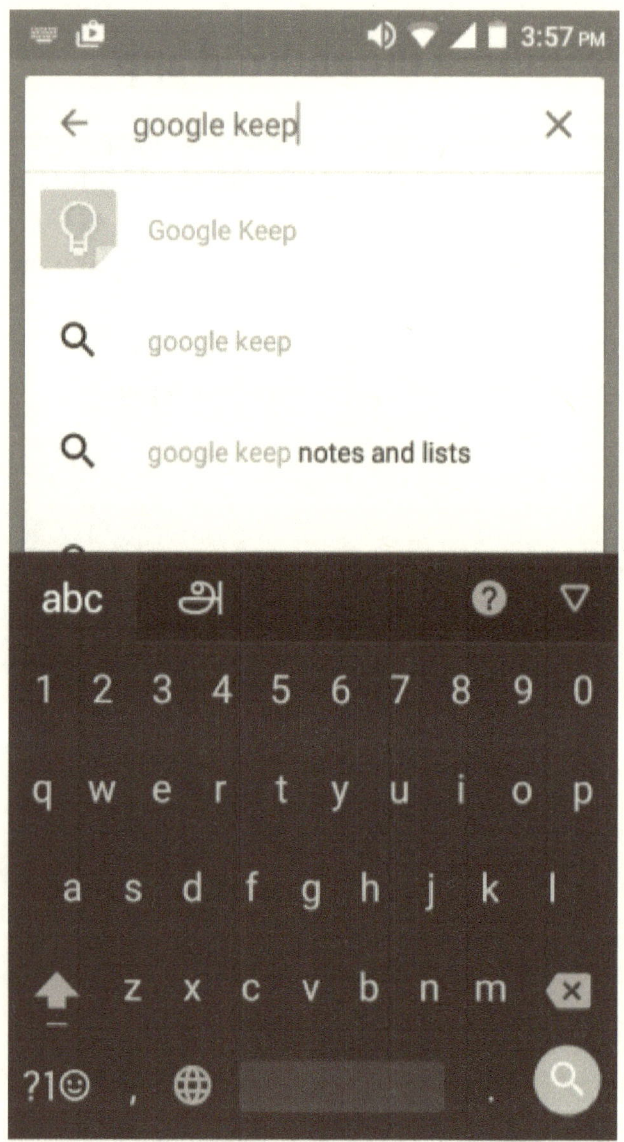
google keep
Google Keep
google keep
google keep notes and lists
abc
?1☺

ALL THAT YOU NEED TO KNOW ABOUT GOOGLE KEEP FOR INCREASING PRODUCTIVITY

Then touch install button.

Wait for it to download and install.

Google Keep

Google Inc.

3+

5.99MB/7.22MB   82%

3:59 PM

Google Keep
Google Inc.
3+
Installing...

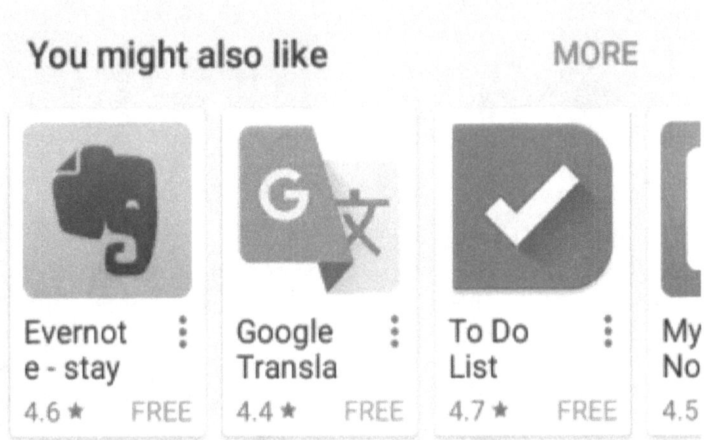
You might also like
MORE
Evernot
e - stay
4.6 ★   FREE
Google
Transla
4.4 ★   FREE
To Do
List
4.7 ★   FREE
My
No
4.5

After installation, you will see the open button (shown below)

Google Keep
Google Inc.

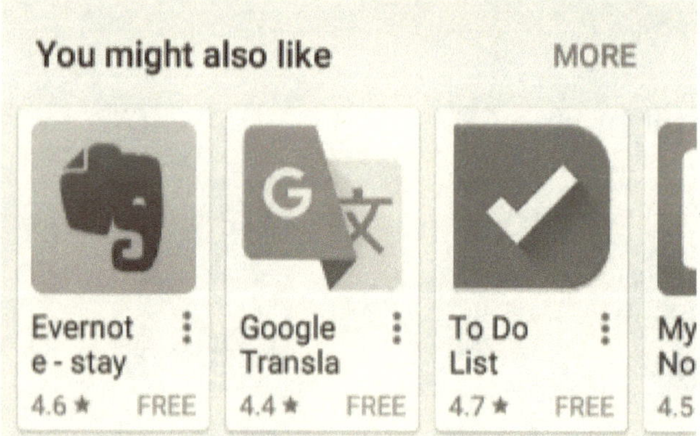

Touch OPEN. Goggle keep account which uses the email you have given for your play store will be loaded.

Click get started.

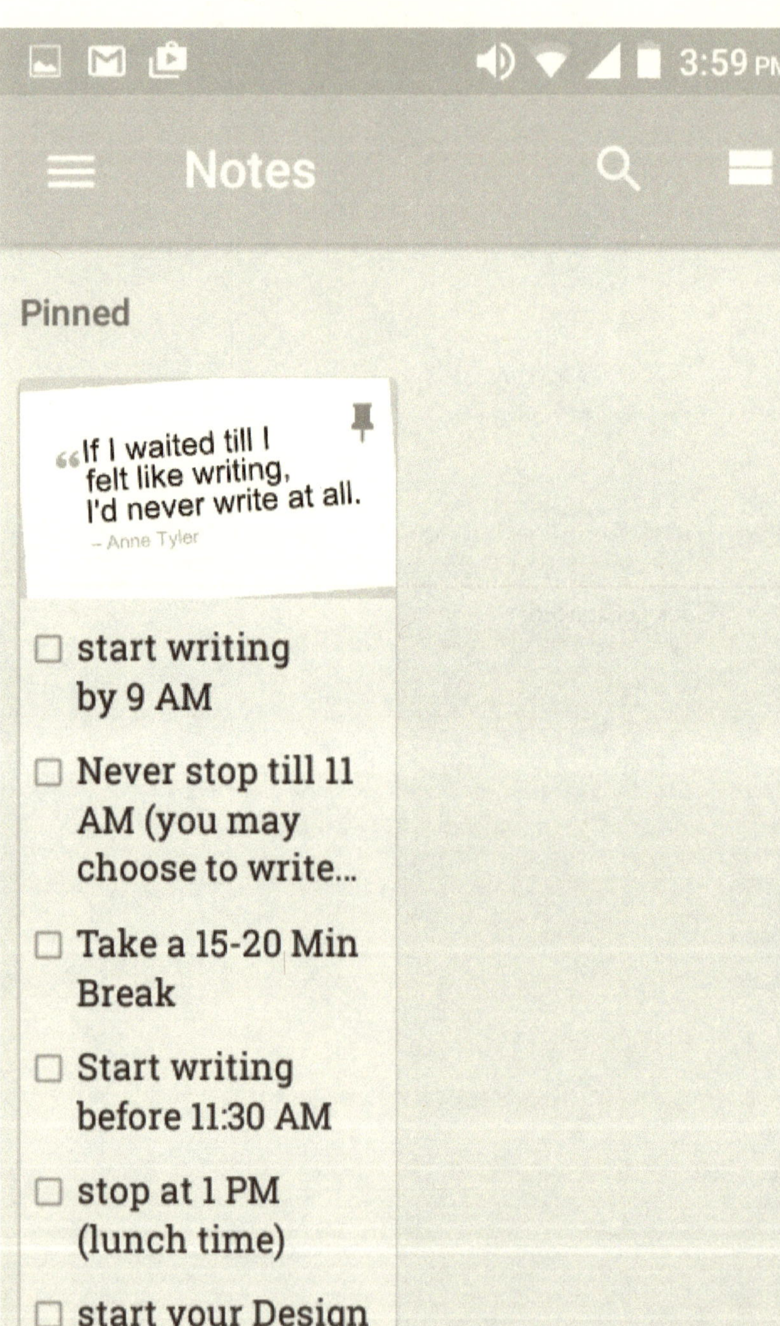

3:59 PM
Notes
Pinned
"If I waited till I felt like writing, I'd never write at all.
-- Anne Tyler
☐ start writing by 9 AM
☐ Never stop till 11 AM (you may choose to write...
☐ Take a 15-20 Min Break
☐ Start writing before 11:30 AM
☐ stop at 1 PM (lunch time)
☐ start your Design works by 2PM
Take a note

ALL THAT YOU NEED TO KNOW ABOUT GOOGLE KEEP FOR INCREASING PRODUCTIVITY

You will see the notes you have already taken.

45

Google keep in Chrome

The chrome browser the Google keep app for chrome and the Google keep extension for chrome. The only difference I can visually see is that it is an app and has a separate window. It is definitely useful for reminders, though.

I already told you I am a Firefox user, when I opened my Google keep account from Google chrome I was surprised to see a new icon in the take a note box.

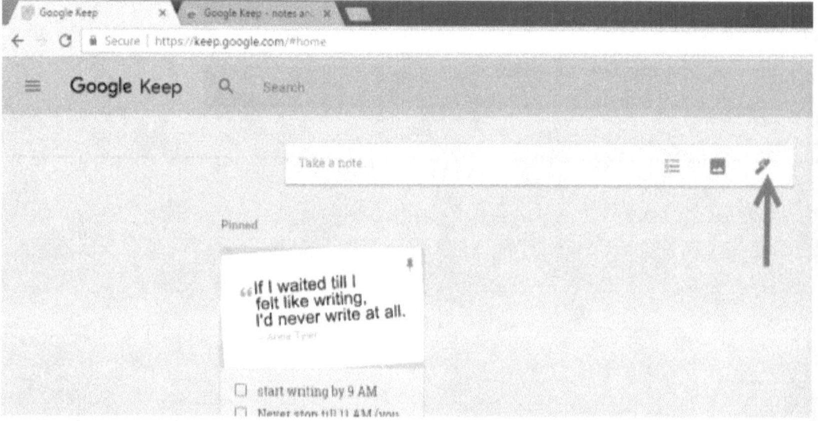

Click that pen like icon and a new window pops up.

ALL THAT YOU NEED TO KNOW ABOUT GOOGLE KEEP FOR INCREASING PRODUCTIVITY

Your online drawing board is now ready for you.

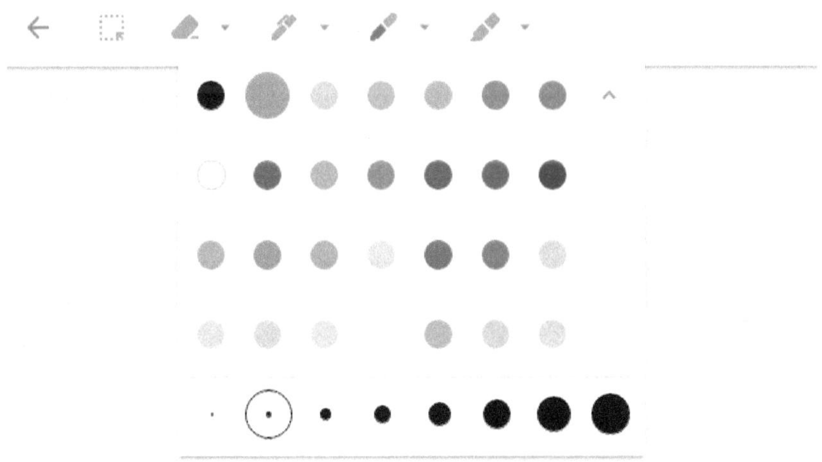

The first icon from the right (the dotted box) is the selection tool for selecting what you have drawn.

The next one to it is the eraser if you click the dropdown arrow near eraser you will see the clear page button.

You can erase the whole drawing in a single click using this button.

Then the next three are different kind of brushes.

You can click the small dropdown arrow icon near any brush and choose the colour and brush thickness.

Try out the different brushes yourself.

Next to the pain brush icons there are three icons.

The undo, redo and full width. Undo & Redo just acts like your ms office's undo and redo.

The full width icon maximizes and reduces the width of the drawing board screen, when clicked.

The last icon in the row is the more options menu.

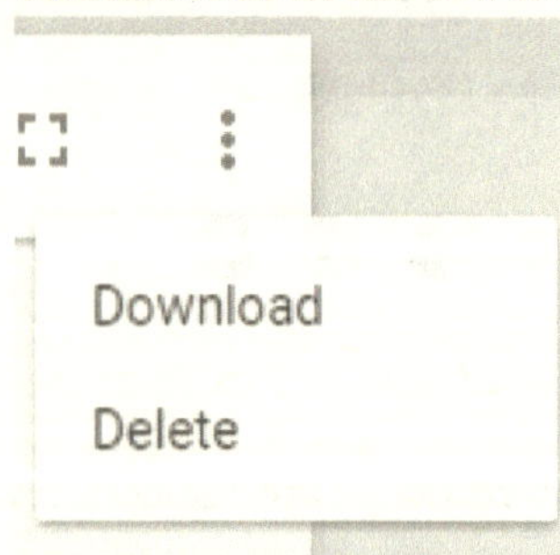

After you draw, if you click the more options icon (the three vertical dots) in the corner, you get two options, download and delete.

Download will download the pic you have drawn to the pc.

Delete will of course delete the drawing.

49

Google keep chrome extension

After successful installation, you will find a small button in the top left corner of your chrome browser

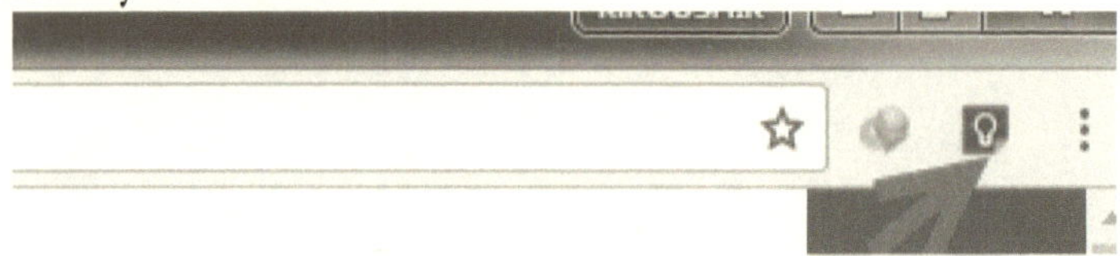

You can click that button to save any website you are visiting to your Google keep as a note.

Let me give you an example

I am searching for 100 online magazines where international writers can apply to write in Google I am in page 3 of the search results, I suddenly get a call and I have to go out to meet a person.

If I can save the page 3 of the results with the last page I saw in it in notes I can continue my search later on.

To do it, all you have to do is click the Google keep button.

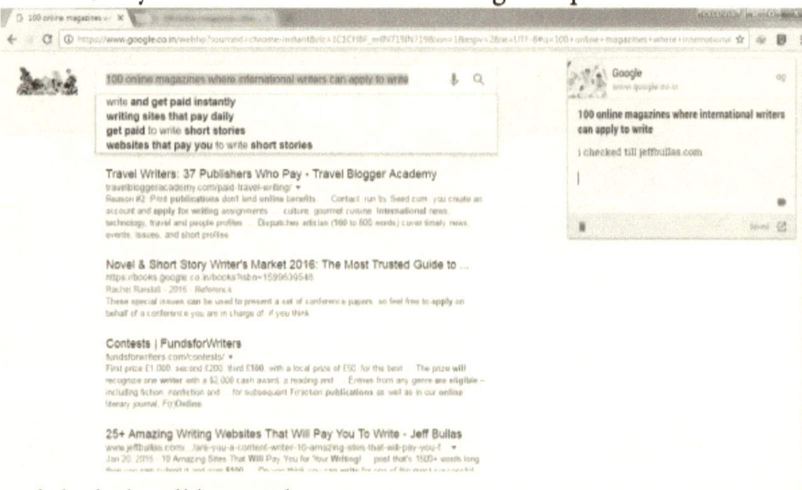

and the link will be saved.

ALL THAT YOU NEED TO KNOW ABOUT GOOGLE KEEP FOR INCREASING PRODUCTIVITY

To make it easily understandable, you can add the search terms in the title and info about till which result (website) you have looked in the notes.

If you have a doubt whether it is saved (since it is the first time you are using)

Visit your Google keep website

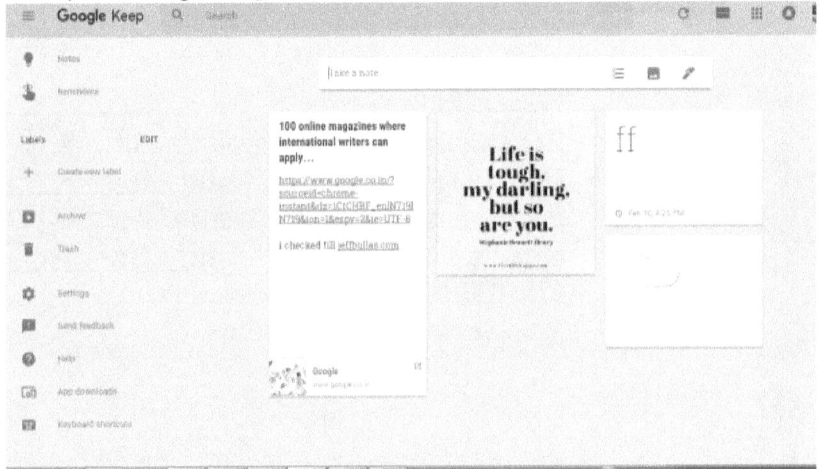

See you find it there.

So you can save any web link as a note with any extra note you type.

Saving selected parts of websites as notes

Let's say you are reading an article and you want to note down a particular paragraph, this extension makes it easy for you,

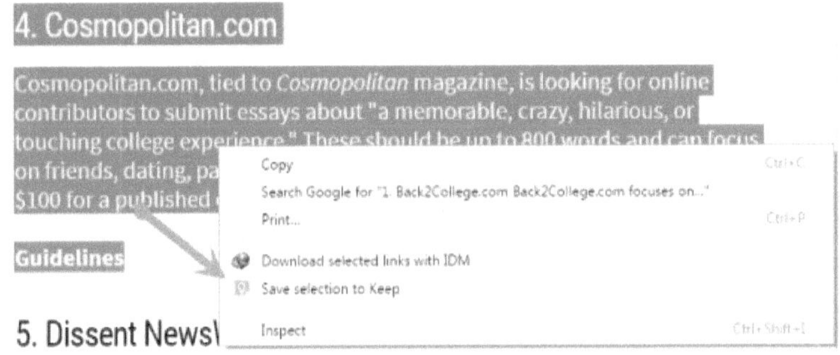

Just select the paragraphs you want to save as a single note.

Right click and then click save selection to keep from the context menu.

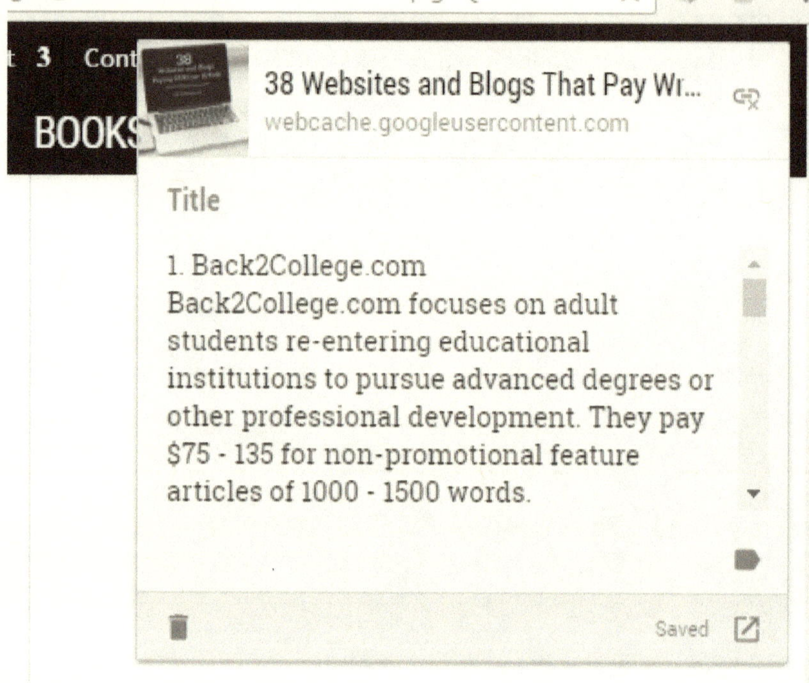

If you want to save different parts of the article to multiple notes, select and then save selection to keep separately.

You can delete the note by pressing the bin icon and add labels by pressing the labels icon.

Saving images to keep

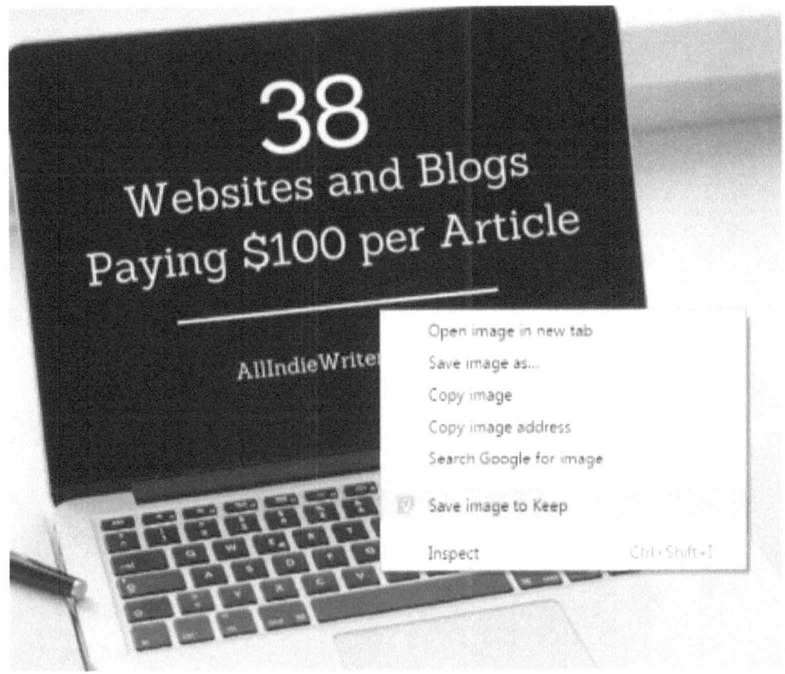

Right click any image you want to save and then select save image to keep.

Now that you have saved whatever you want to as notes, you can do everything you do with a normal note from your Google keep app or by visiting keep.google.com and logging in.

Google Keep in Android

54

Taking voice notes

You can also note a new microphone icon. (Which you have not seen in your pc)

Click it to take voice notes

If you click it but don't speak anything you will see the below
screen.

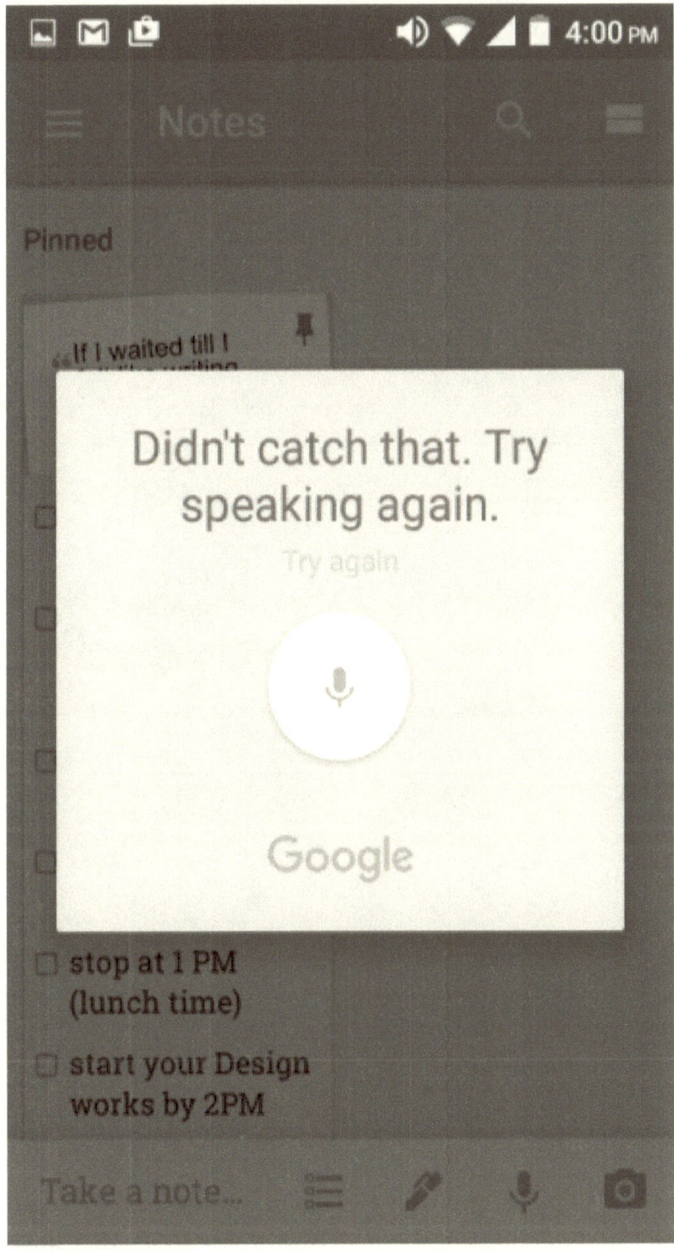

Tap the mic button again to start speaking.

See I created my first voice note. You are able to see that my voice is already transcribed in to text. (With no punctuations though, but I can always correct it.

The audio file is also attached to the note.

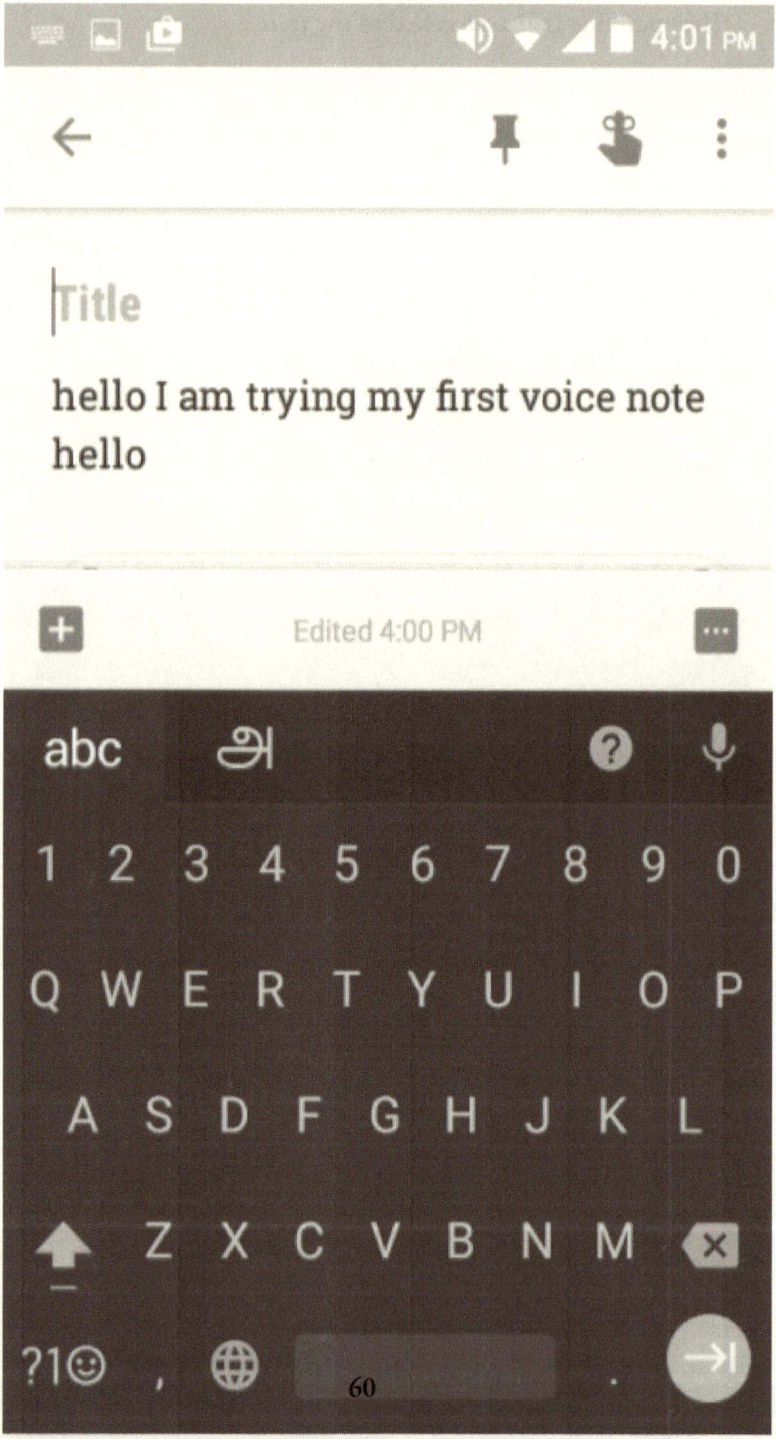

4:01 PM
Title
hello I am trying my first voice note hello
Edited 4:00 PM
abc
1 2 3 4 5 6 7 8 9 0
Q W E R T Y U I O P
A S D F G H J K L
Z X C V B N M
?1☺

You can give a title.

61

ALL THAT YOU NEED TO KNOW ABOUT GOOGLE KEEP FOR
INCREASING PRODUCTIVITY

Below any note, you will see a plus button in the bottom right corner and three horizontal ... (three dots) button in the bottom left corner.

4:02 PM

Test voice4

hello I am trying my first voice note hello

0:13

Take photo

Choose image

Drawing

Recording

Checkboxes

Edited 4:02 PM

Clicking the plus button you can add different things to a note. Like image, drawing, recording or check boxes. (When you add check boxes the entire note turns in to an item list. (Same as is Google keep website)

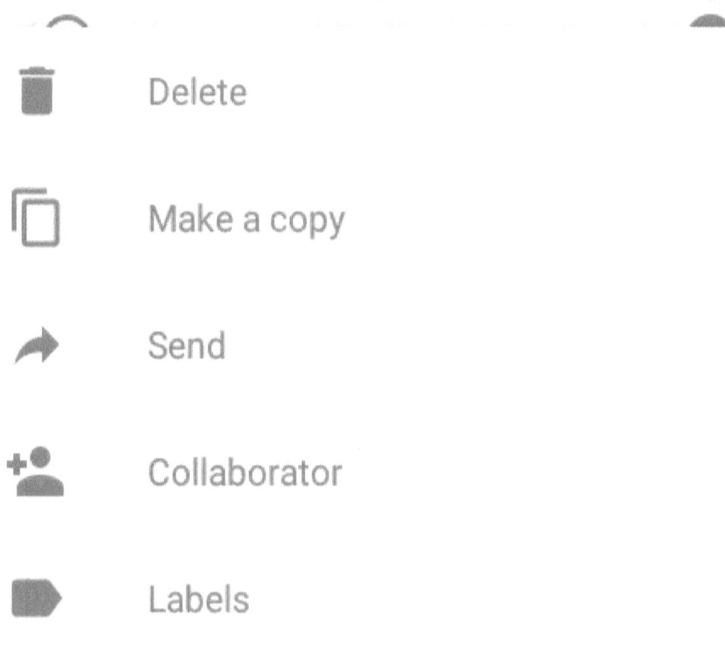
4:02 PM
Test voice4
hello I am trying my first voice note hello
Delete
Make a copy
Send
Collaborator
Labels
Edited 4:02 PM

The three horizontal dots button is the more options button, by clicking it you get the menu having delete, make a copy, send collaborator, labels and colours.

You can also download the audio in to your mobile or pc or laptop if you want to.

Send in more options

If you touch the more options button of any note, you will get send as one of the options.

Touch send.

A box will pop up with two options

Copy to Google doc.

Send through other apps.

Touch send through other apps,

You will see a list of apps,

You can scroll up and down to see the full list

Touch any of the app to use the send functionality of that app to send this particular note to that app

For example, if you choose Gmail, Gmail will a blank message will be created with the note on its body text.

If you touch Google hangouts from the list, it will ask you to select the recipient and will send it to them.

Adding a reminder using keep android app.

Adding a reminder is slightly different (in look and feel) in android app. Let us see that also

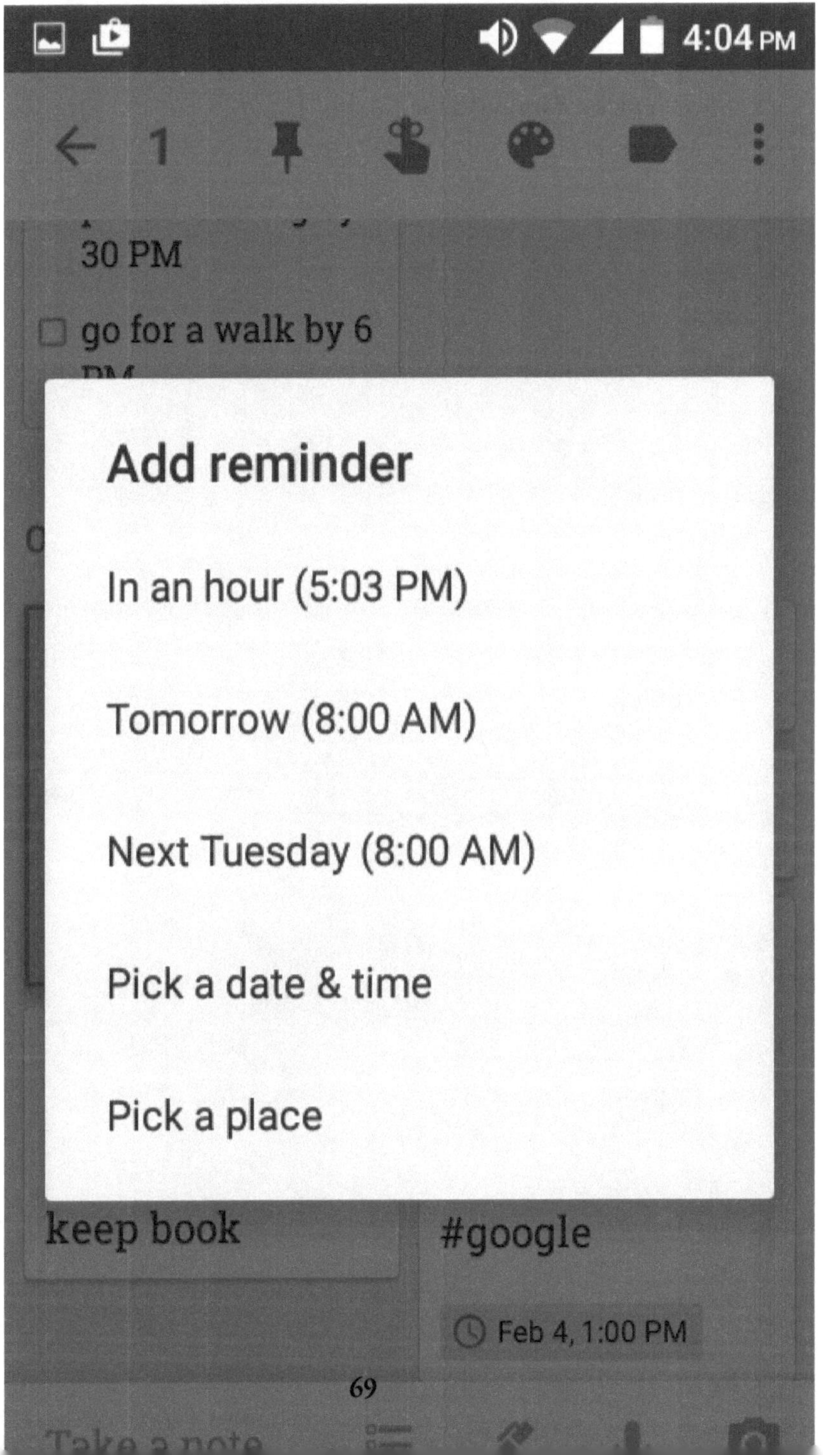
4:04 PM
1
30 PM
go for a walk by 6
PM
Add reminder
In an hour (5:03 PM)
Tomorrow (8:00 AM)
Next Tuesday (8:00 AM)
Pick a date & time
Pick a place
keep book
#google
Feb 4, 1:00 PM
Take a note

Select a note and click reminder, you will see the above box popping up

Touch pick a date and time.

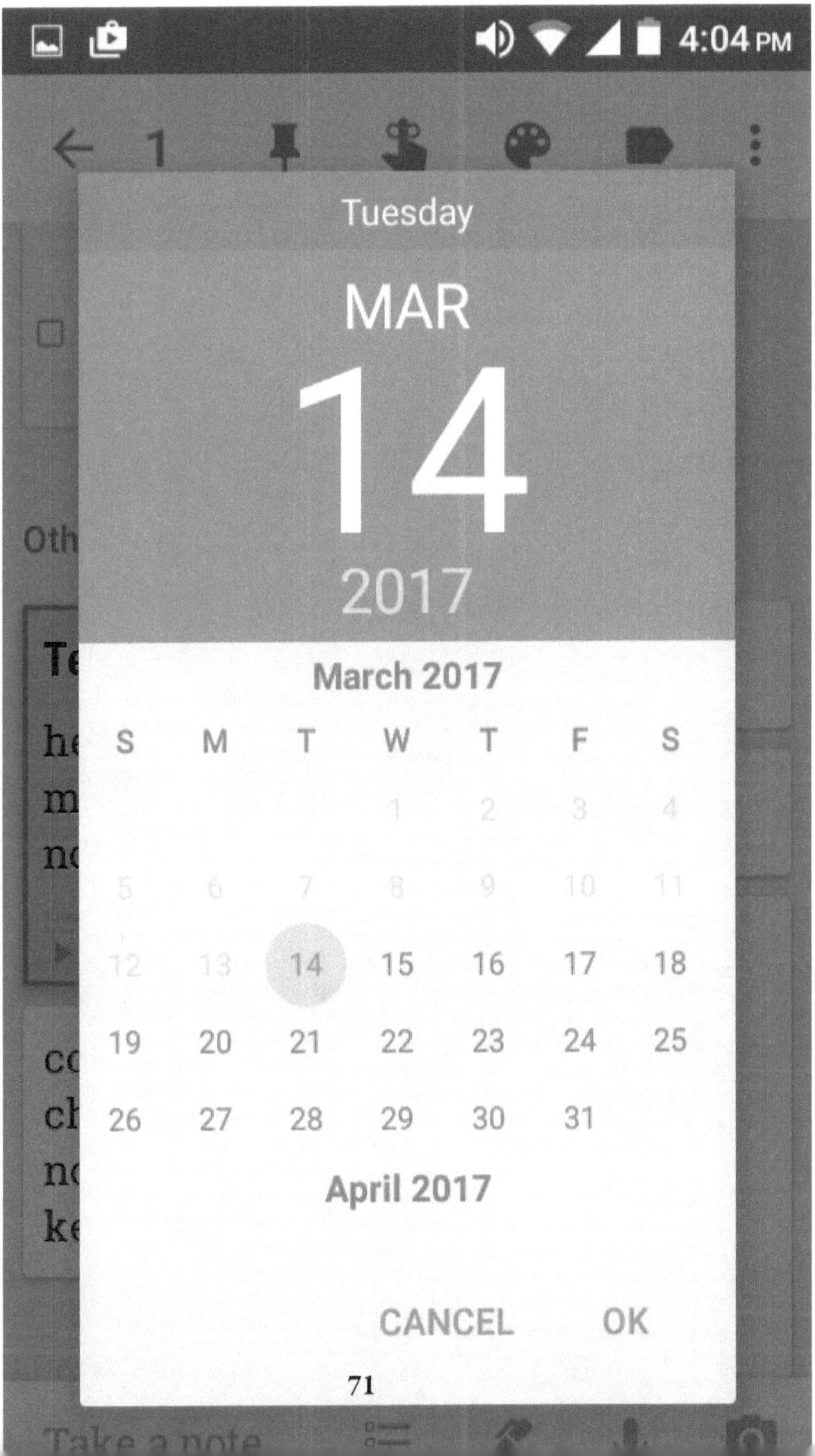
4:04 PM
1
Tuesday
MAR
14
2017
March 2017
S M T W T F S
1 2 3 4
5 6 7 8 9 10 11
12 13 14 15 16 17 18
19 20 21 22 23 24 25
26 27 28 29 30 31
April 2017
CANCEL
OK
Take a note

KOUSHIK K

Select a date and click ok.

4:04 PM
1
5:00 AM PM
12
11
1
10
2
9
3
8
4
7
5
6
CANCEL   OK

KOUSHIK K

Select the hour by adjusting the hour clock. Drag the green circle with your finger and click ok.

4:30 AM PM
00
55 05
50 10
45 15
40 20
35 25
30
CANCEL OK
Take a note...

Set time in your minute clock too by dragging the green circle.
Then click ok
I have set my reminder to 4:30 pm today (now it is 4 pm)

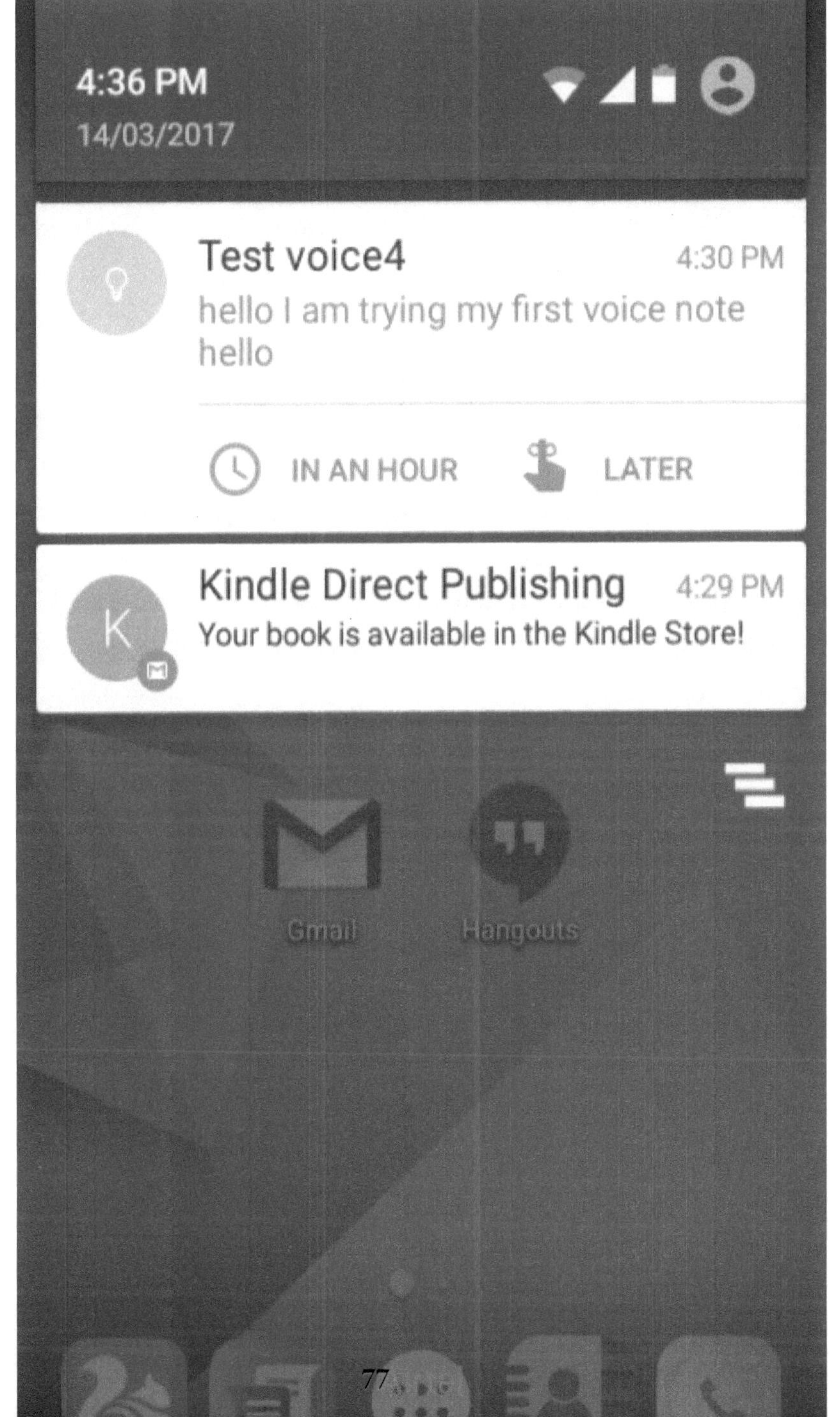
4:36 PM
14/03/2017
Test voice4
4:30 PM
hello I am trying my first voice note hello
IN AN HOUR
LATER
Kindle Direct Publishing
4:29 PM
Your book is available in the Kindle Store!
Gmail
Hangouts

Wow I got a reminder in my mobile, by 4:30 PM, with tone.

Now the only disadvantage is you don't have a separate tone settings for Google keep. It will play the default tone you have set for all your notifications. . So there is a chance, that you may ignore the reminder thinking it is a message.

Oh yes this is a very big disadvantage, don't worry, we have third party apps to solve it.

Notification catch app

https://play.google.com/store/apps/details?id=antx.tools.catchnotification

This app offers the feature to add different sounds for different app's notifications.

There is only one limitation to this app which is you can only set a custom ring tone for any one app.

Though this is a big limitation I am okay with it because all I need is to set a different notification to Google keep's notifications.

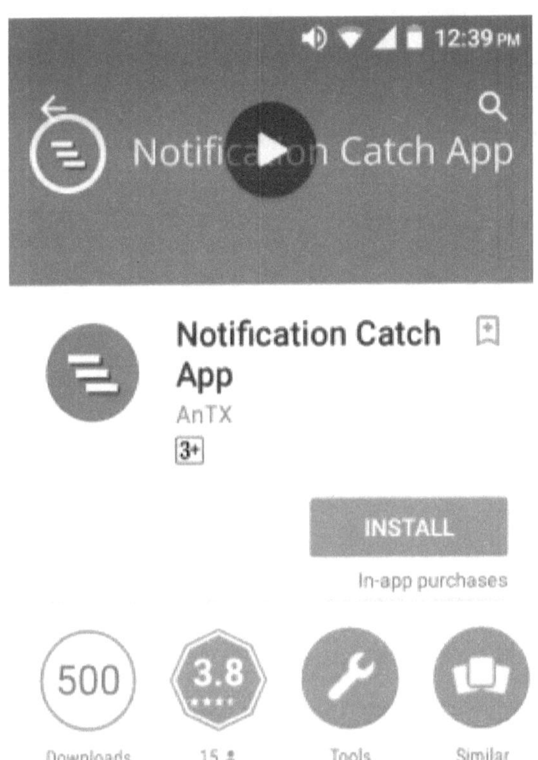

Open the above given link in your android phone. Click install.

Notification Catch App

12:39 PM
Notification Catch App
needs access to
$ In-app purchases
Identity
Photos/Media/Files
Device ID & call information
Google Play   ACCEPT
Use Notification Catch App
READ MORE

A screen will popup, Click accept

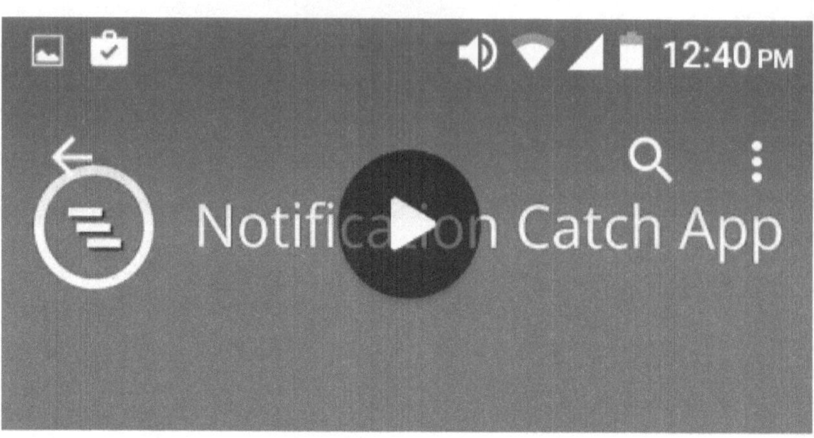

Notification Catch App

AnTX

3+

UNINSTALL   OPEN

In-app purchases

You might also like

MORE

Pest Control	Sound Profile	Smart Notify -	Vib n
5.0 ★ FREE	4.2 ★ FREE	4.4 ★ FREE	4.1

After it downloads and installs, you will see the above screen. Click open

Notification Catch App – Privacy Policy

INTRODUCTION
Welcome to Notification Catch App!
We value your privacy. This Privacy Policy informs you of your choices and our practices regarding any Information (as defined in the The Information We Collect section below) you provide to us.
The use of Notification Catch App (through the Notification Catch App mobile app) may involve the collection and use of your Information. It is important for you to understand how this happens and how you may control it, so please read this Privacy Policy carefully.
By using Notification Catch App,

84DECLINE   ACCEPT

Privacy policy text will be displayed read it well and decide whether you want to use this app. (I am okay with it) click accept if you want to use the app.

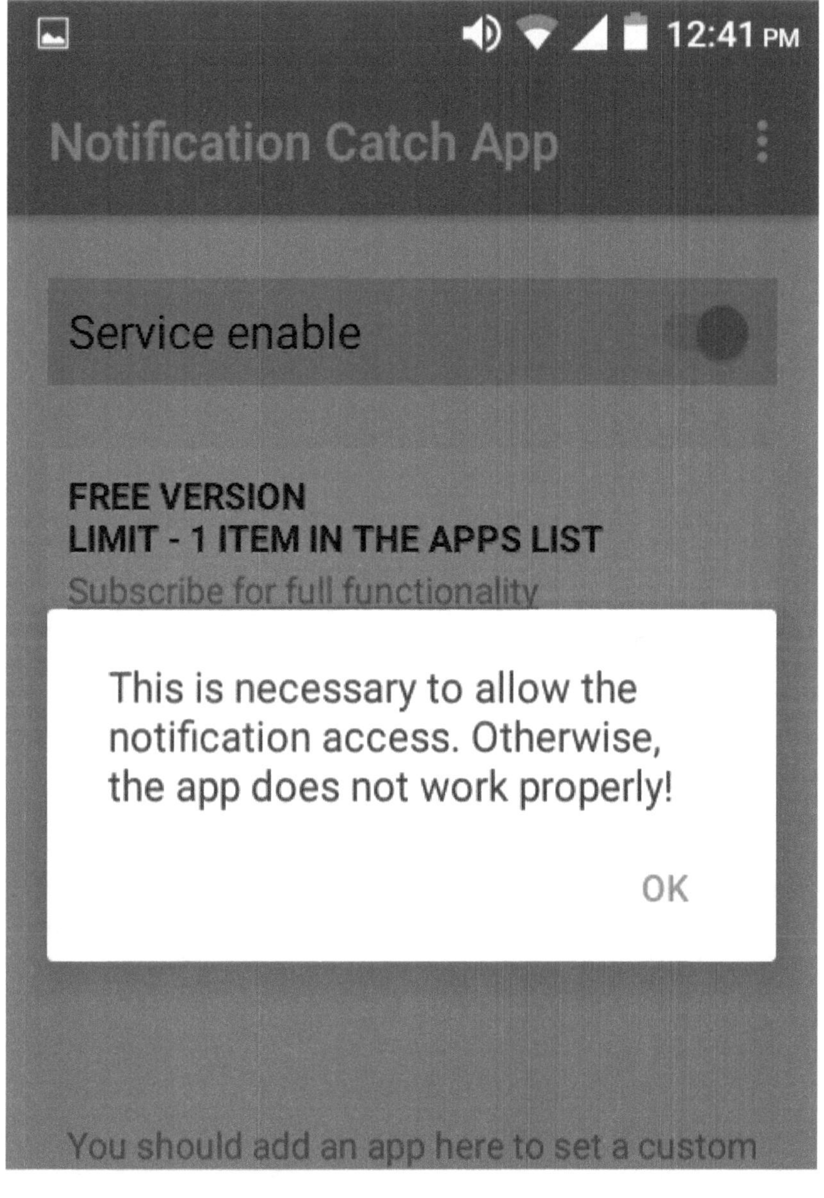

A message box will pop up, click ok you will be taken to the notification access settings of your phone.

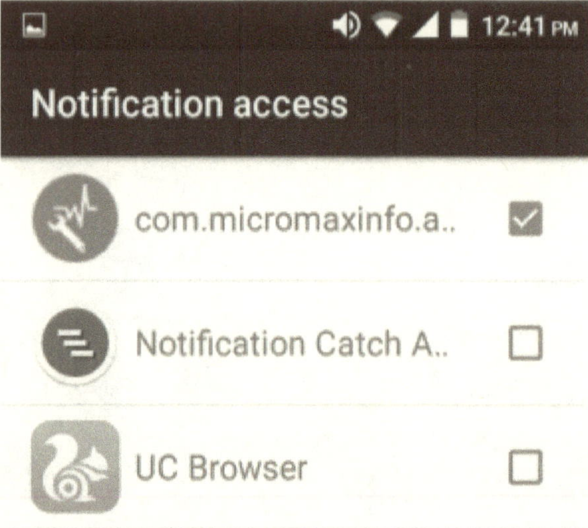

Tick the notification catch app checkbox. The first check box is ticked by default, don't uncheck that.
Touch the back button.

Notification Catch App
12:42 PM

Service enable

FREE VERSION
LIMIT - 1 ITEM IN THE APPS LIST
Subscribe for full functionality

APPS   SOUND PROFILES

You should add an app here to set a custom
sound to it's notifications

You will see the above screen. Touch the sign.

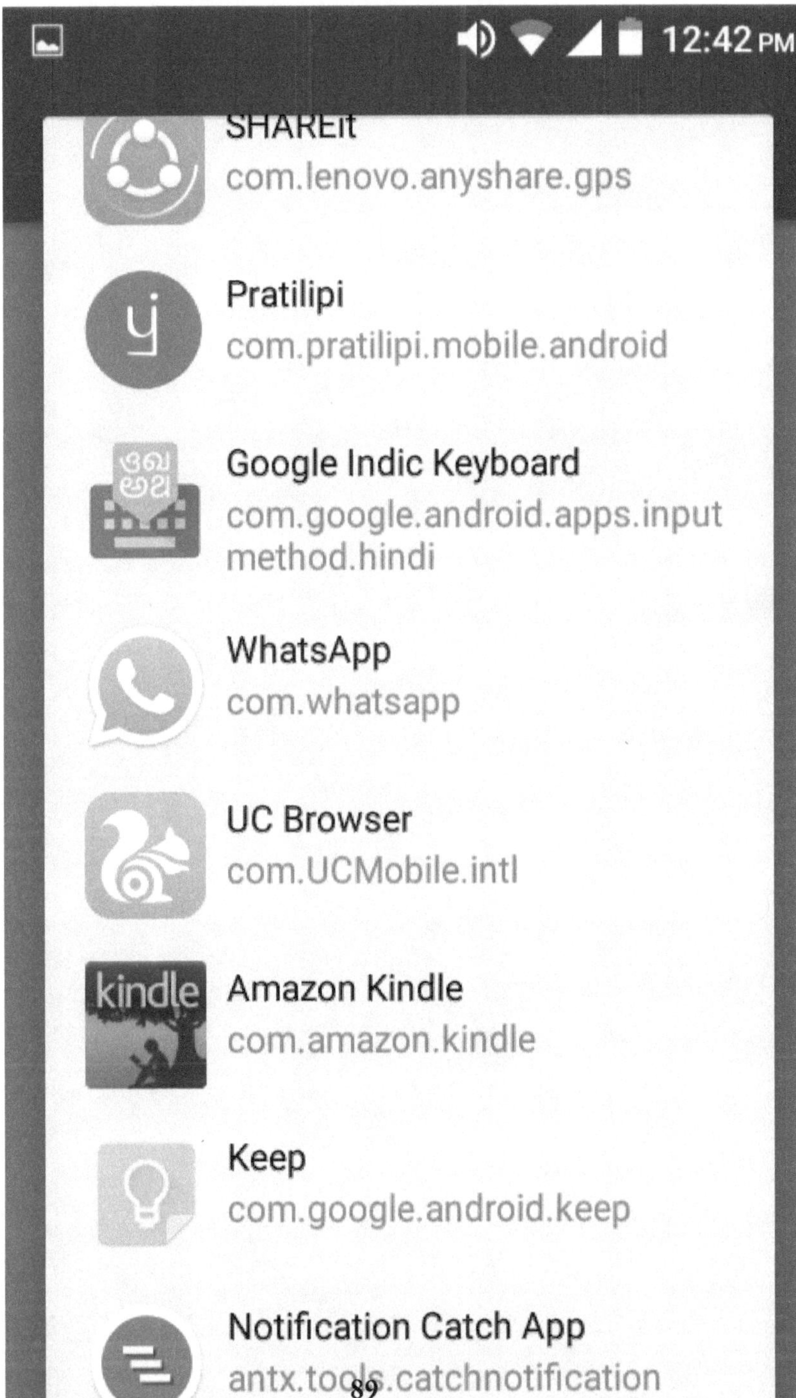
12:42 PM
SHAREit
com.lenovo.anyshare.gps
Pratilipi
com.pratilipi.mobile.android
Google Indic Keyboard
com.google.android.apps.input
method.hindi
WhatsApp
com.whatsapp
UC Browser
com.UCMobile.intl
Amazon Kindle
com.amazon.kindle
Keep
com.google.android.keep
Notification Catch App
antx.tools.catchnotification

KOUSHIK K

Select keep from the list of apps, by touching it.

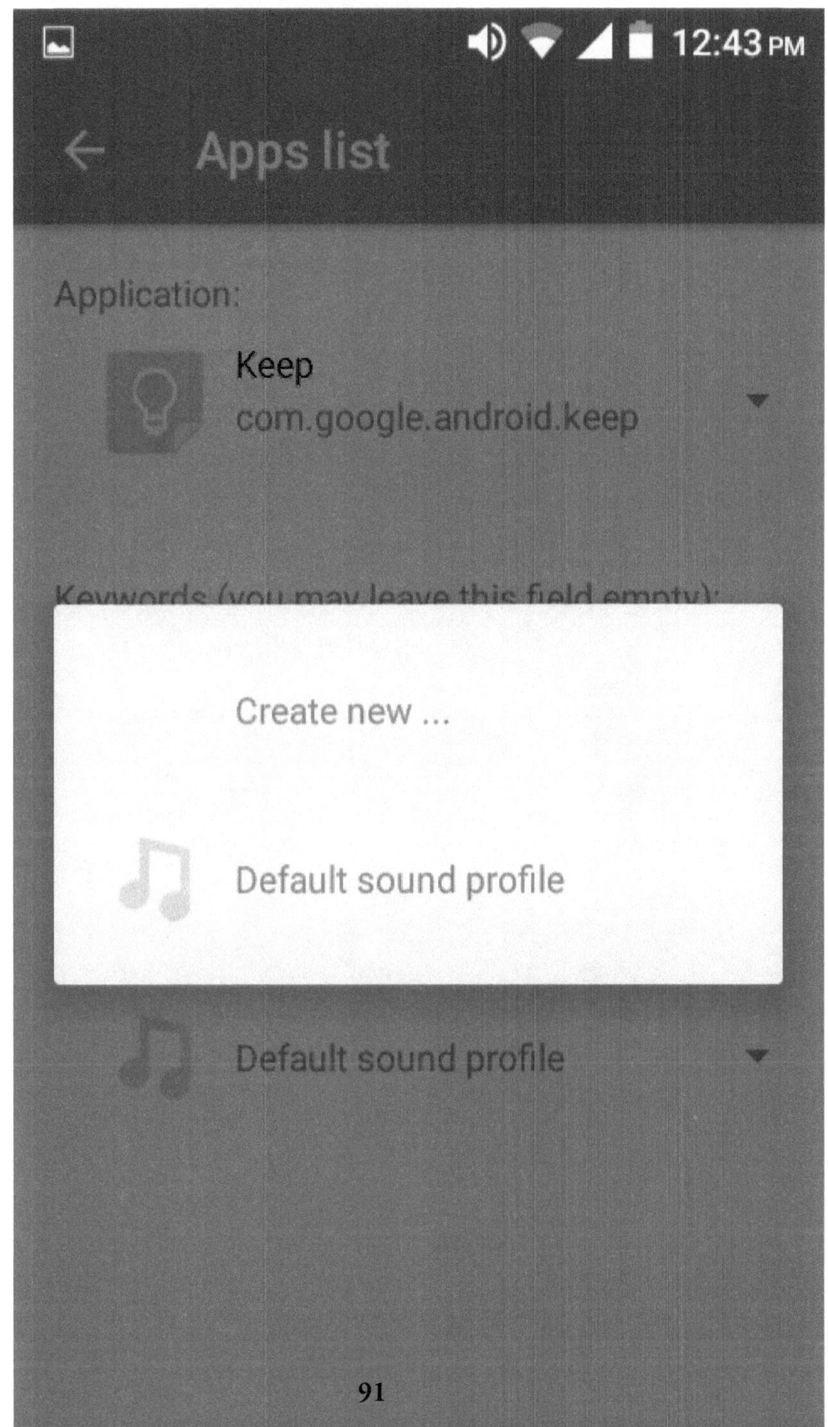
Apps list
Application:
Keep
com.google.android.keep
Keywords (you may leave this field empty):
Create new ...
Default sound profile
Default sound profile
12:43 PM

Touch the default sound profile and a box will popup. Touch create new.... link.

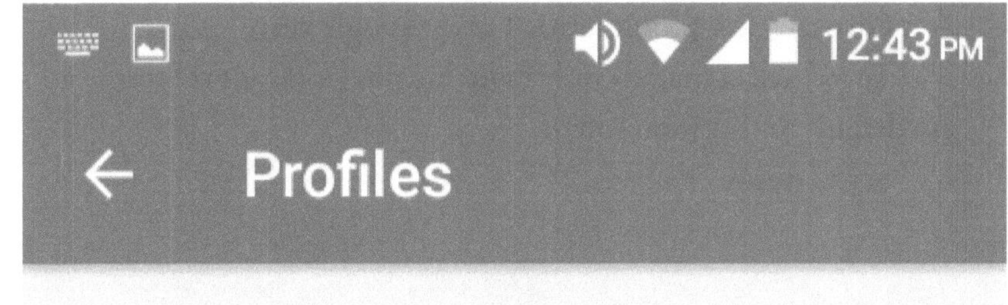
12:43 PM
Profiles
Profile name:
Google keep
melody only   alert and melody
vibration
Jeep   keeping   jeep   keeps
1 2 3 4 5 6 7 8 9 0
q w e r t y u i o p
a s d f g h j k l
z x c v b n m
?1☺

Give the new profile a title I gave Google keep.

Then I select melody only radio button (it means ringtone only and no default notification sound.

Scroll down

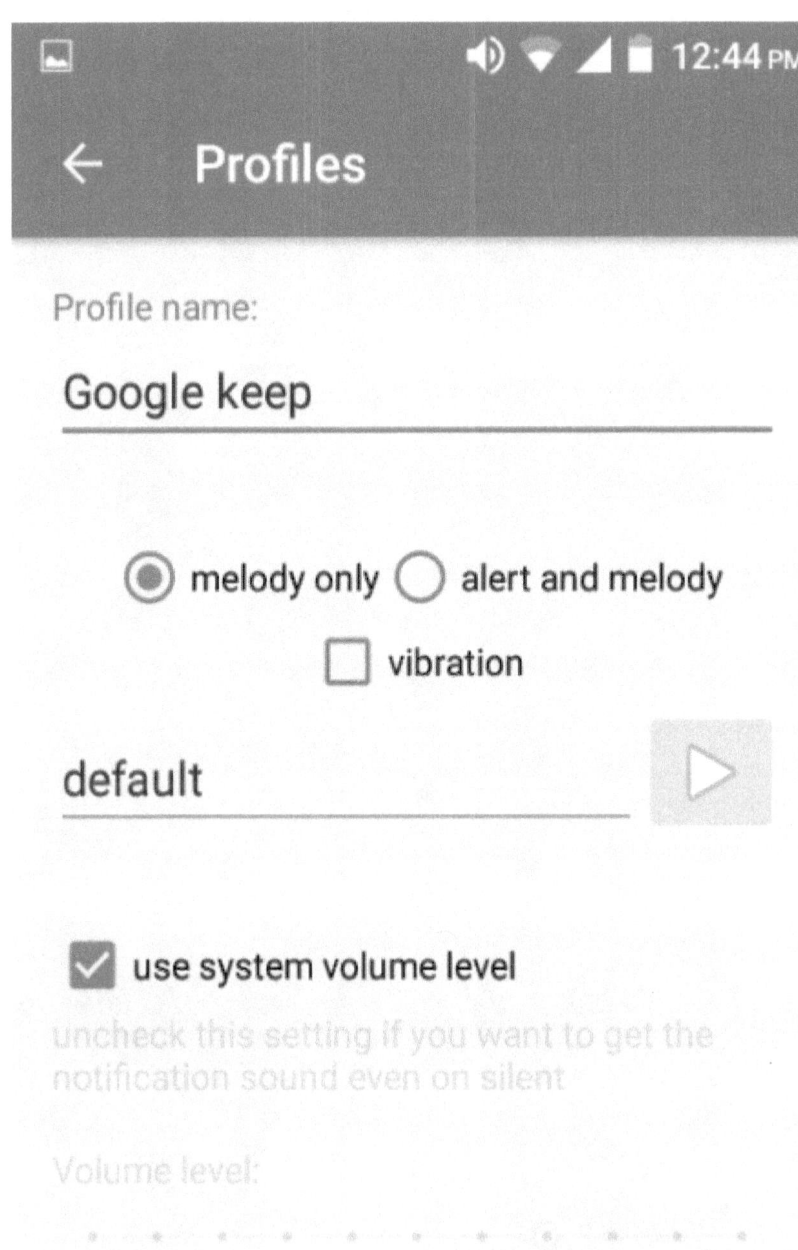
Profiles
Profile name:
Google keep
melody only   alert and melody
vibration
default
use system volume level
uncheck this setting if you want to get the
notification sound even on silent
Volume level:

Tap the default ringtone

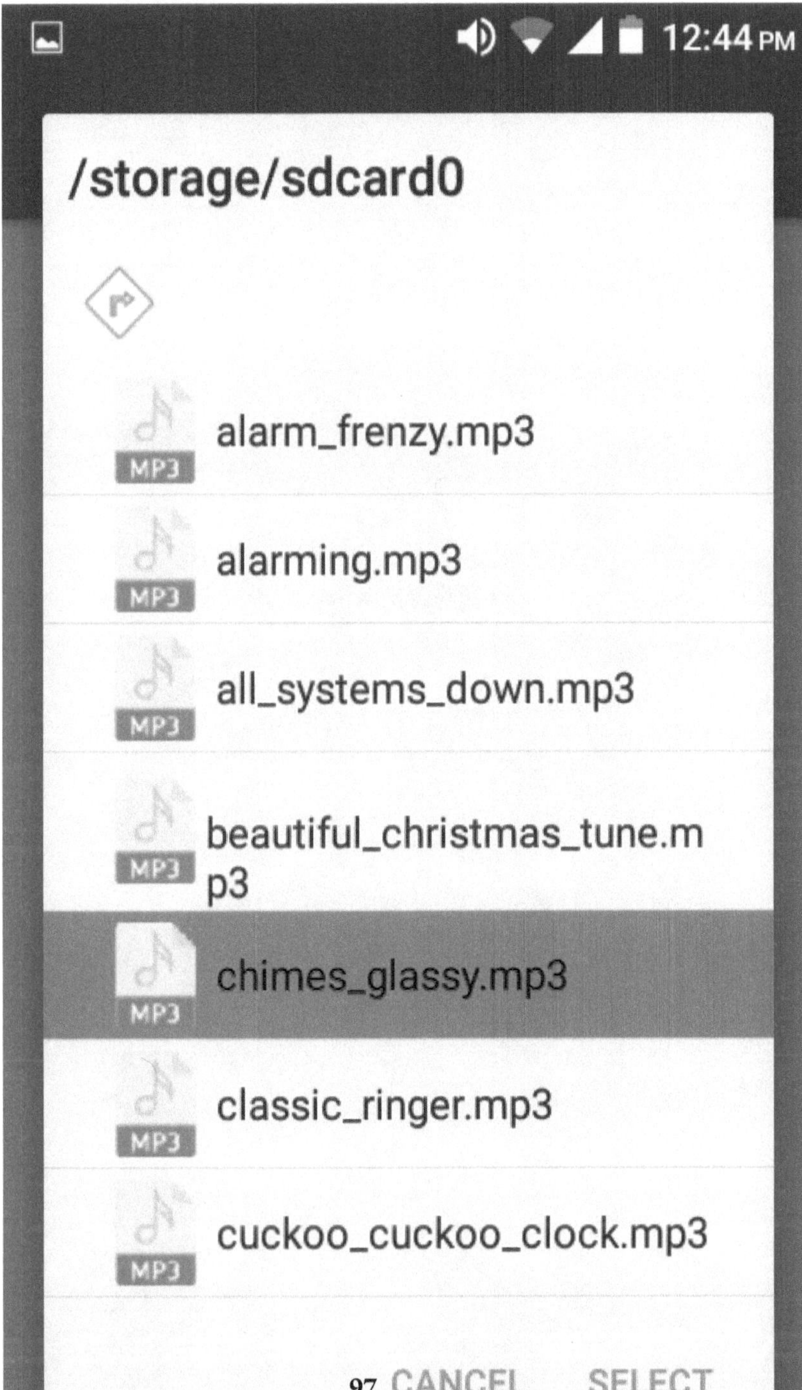
12:44 PM
/storage/sdcard0
alarm_frenzy.mp3
MP3
alarming.mp3
MP3
all_systems_down.mp3
MP3
beautiful_christmas_tune.m
MP3
p3
chimes_glassy.mp3
MP3
classic_ringer.mp3
MP3
cuckoo_cuckoo_clock.mp3
MP3
CANCEL
SELECT

KOUSHIK K

Touch a tone from the list to choose and then touch SELECT

98

Touch a tone from the list to choose and then touch SELECT

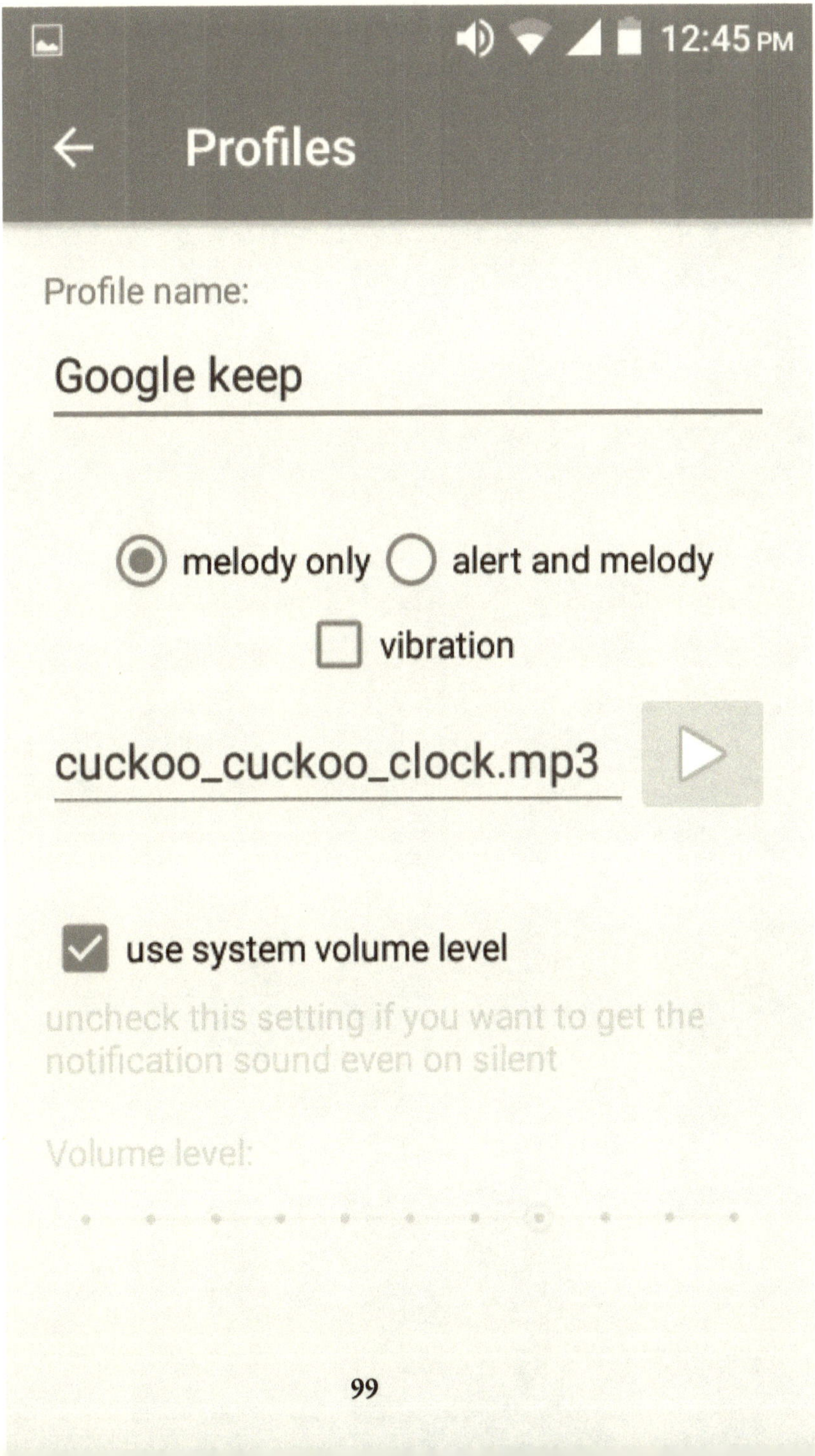

12:45 PM
Profiles
Profile name:
Google keep
melody only   alert and melody
vibration
cuckoo_cuckoo_clock.mp3
use system volume level
uncheck this setting if you want to get the notification sound even on silent
Volume level:

Now the tone you chose shows in the place of ringtone.
Touch the back arrow button.

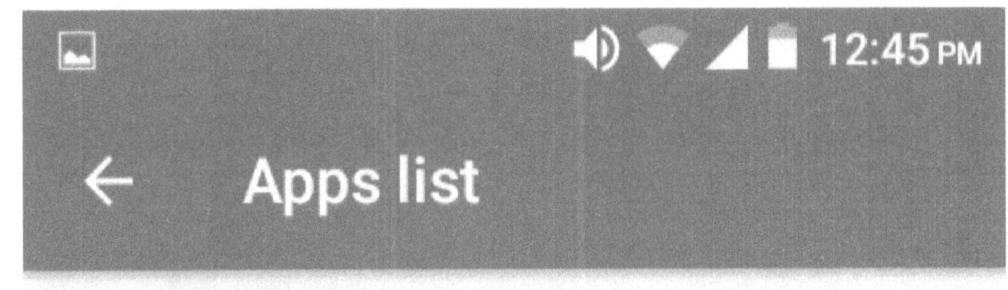
12:45 PM
Apps list

Application:

Keep
com.google.android.keep

Keywords (you may leave this field empty):

The sound profile will apply, if notification contains this keywords.

Sound profile:

Google keep

You can see that the sound profile which is currently loaded for Google keep is goggle keep (the profile created by you.
Touch the home button and come out. You are done.

Sharing notes from other application

You can share notes from any other notes app or any application to Google keep.

Let me show you with the help of my default notes application of my mobile.

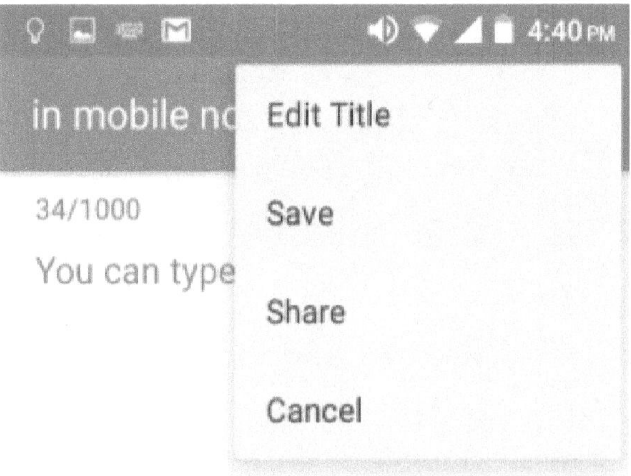

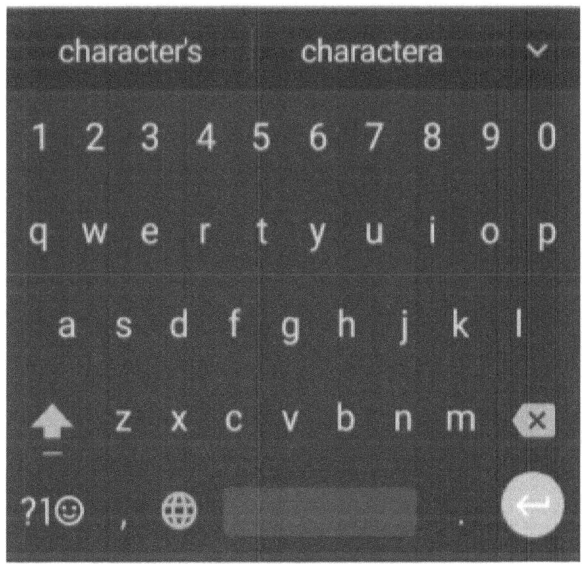

I select a note from my notes app and click share.

104

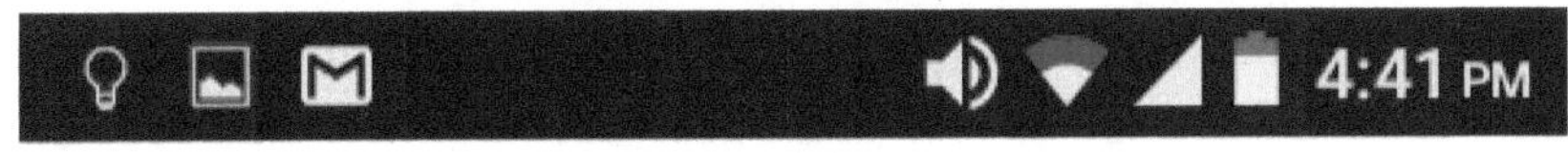

Share:in mobile note
WhatsApp
Messaging
Gmail
Hangouts
Messenger
SMS
SHAREit
Keep

See that keep is shown in your share menu. You can use the share button of any app to share notes to your keep. (Sharing to keep just saves the note to Google keep)

Searching for notes

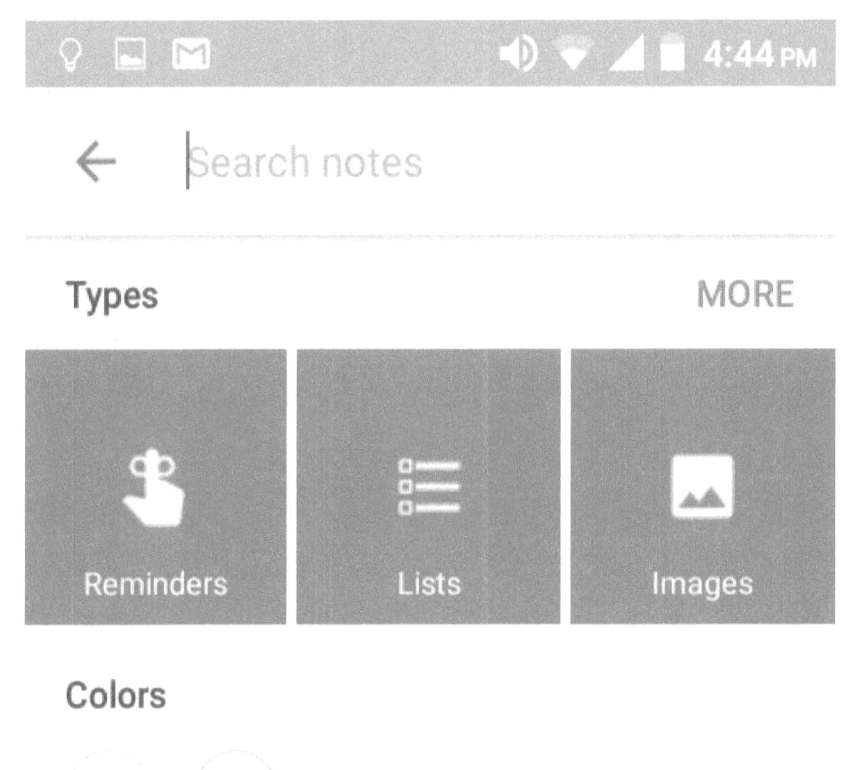

You can search your notes by typing keywords or you can filter them by type. (I have three types created. But there are more types)

You can filter the notes by the colour you gave to them

Photo and images

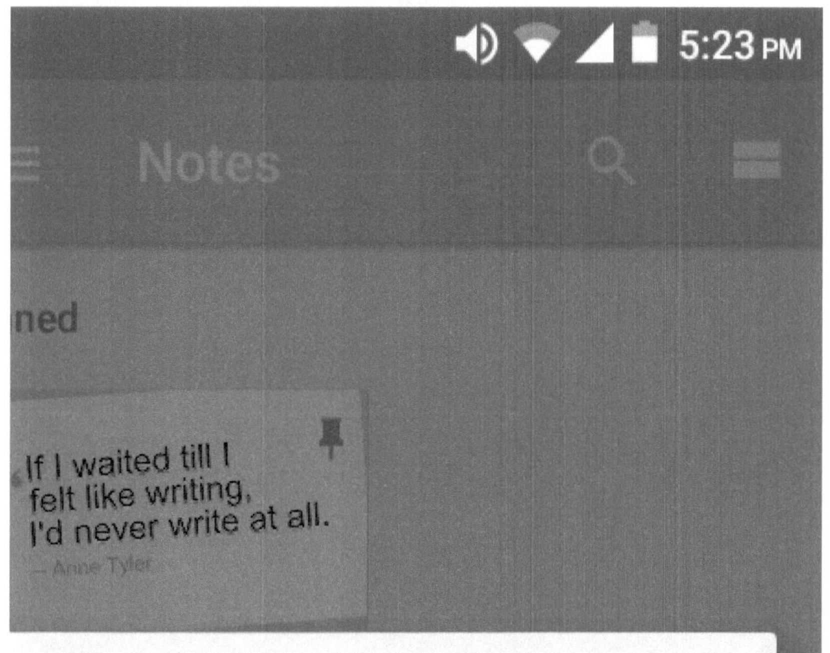
5:23 PM
Notes
If I waited till I
felt like writing,
I'd never write at all.
— Anne Tyler
Add image
Take photo
Choose image
Start writing
before 11:30 AM
stop at 1 PM
(lunch time)
start your Design

109

You can take a photo from your phone, or upload an image. This feature is also available in web version and hence I am not elaborating on it.

Grabbing text from Images

Tap any image in a note to go to a similar screen as shown above.

Touch the three vertical dots (more option button) on the top left corner of the screen.

ALL THAT YOU NEED TO KNOW ABOUT GOOGLE KEEP FOR INCREASING PRODUCTIVITY

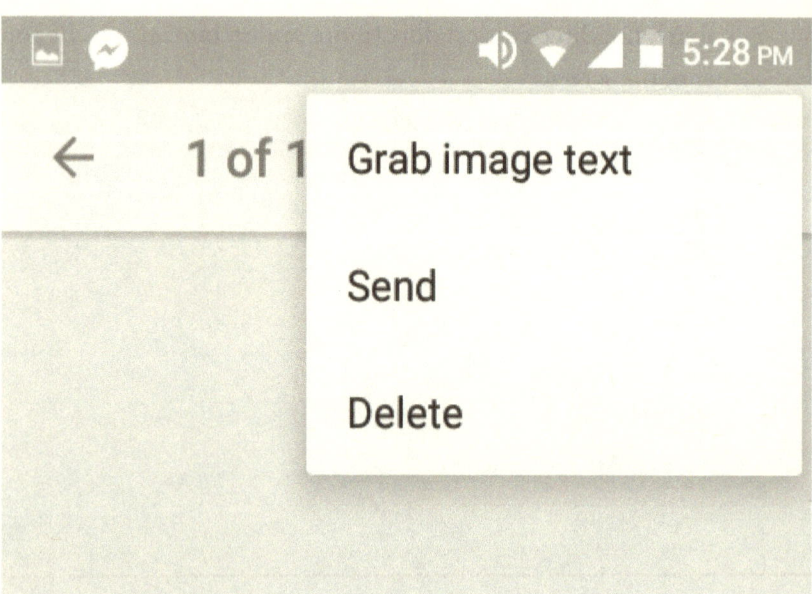

"If I waited till I felt like writing, I'd never write at all.

— Anne Tyler

Touch grab image text.

Title

If I waited till I
felt like writing,
I'd never write at all.
Anne Tyler

Edited 5:30 PM

You are done grabbing the text. Give a title and add anything you want to the note.

The next steps

Now you know all the features of Google keep. Just have to start using it in your life practically and it will definitely make your life and work easier.

Google may introduce more features in to keep in future and I will try my best to keep this book up to date for you.

All the best.

Contact Me:

You can always feel free to contact me or send me suggestions, doubts to writetokoushik@yahoo.com

You can also visit my blog to keep in touch with me authorkoushik.tumblr.com[1]

1.   http://authorkoushik.tumblr.com

Please Leave a Review

Thank you for reading the book. Hope you enjoyed it.

If you like this book and enjoyed reading, it would be really helpful if you can share your experience by **leaving a review**

If you have had any problems with the book, please feel free to message me through email writetokoushik@yahoo.com

I will try my best to help you with it.

Thank you

K.koushik

Other Books by Author

Tales of Hanuman
Tales of Hanuman vol 2
Hanuman Chalisa Explained
The Heart of Sun God - A Hymn from Valmiki Ramayana
Durga Saptashloki The Seven Verses from Devi Mahathmyam
19 PLUS TIPS FOR USING GMAIL TO THE FULLEST
Who Should Start a Membership Business
All that you need to know When Buying Domains
All that you need to know About tumblr Blogs
Glories of Shiva: Kaalahastheeshwara (coming soon)
Glories of Shiva: Stories from the Shiva Mahimna Stotra (coming soon)

Visit my blog : authorkoushik.tumblr.com to buy my books

Don't miss out!

Visit the website below and you can sign up to receive emails whenever Koushik K publishes a new book. There's no charge and no obligation.

https://books2read.com/r/B-A-WUEE-ZJCN

BOOKS 2 READ

Connecting independent readers to independent writers.